PICKING UP THE PIECES:
LIFE
AFTER CANCER

CLAIRE BRISSETTE-LAMOUREUX. Ph.D.

BALBOA.
PRESS
A DIVISION OF HAY HOUSE

Balboa Press books may be ordered through booksellers or by contacting:

Balboa Press
A Division of Hay House
1663 Liberty Drive
Bloomington, IN 47403
www.balboapress.com
1 (877) 407-4847

Print information available on the last page.

ISBN: 978-1-5043-3642-0 (sc)
ISBN: 978-1-5043-3643-7 (e)

Library of Congress Control Number: 2015910828

Balboa Press rev. date: 07/31/2015

TO MY MOTHER, CLAIRE (D.1991)
MY SISTERS, JEANNE (D. 1990) AND ANNE (D. 1997)
MY DEAR FRIEND, MARY (D. 1986)
WHO LIVED THEIR DYING WITH
COURAGE, DIGNITY AND FAITH

TO ALL CANCER SURVIVORS
AS WE LIVE TODAY IN GRATITUDE AND HOPE

CONTENTS

INTRODUCTION

In 2004, at age 64, I was diagnosed with bi-lateral breast cancer. I was devastated! Suddenly, and without warning, my life was turned upside-down. I was frightened, terrified, confused, shocked. How could this happen after so many years of living a healthy life-style? It made no sense!

Cancer breaks into our lives unexpectedly. It is a shocking and traumatizing life crisis. It plunges us into an unknown world, where the name of the game is survival---getting through multiple tests and doctor visits, surviving surgery and/or treatment, with an outcome that is often not clear. Generally, we tend to receive very good medical care and follow-up from oncology specialists. However, moving on from the experience of cancer and all that it entails, does not end after the last treatment or after having recuperated from surgery.

The experience of cancer affects us on every level. It changes our sense of self. It shifts our priorities. While the medical profession focuses on physical treatment, not much is said or written about the emotional, psychological and spiritual dimensions of the cancer experience. We are not often encouraged to seek out support groups. We tend to keep to ourselves, not wanting to burden family and friends. For the most part, we are left to our own devices to pick up the pieces of our life.

Living through cancer can become an opportunity to look within. The crisis of cancer invites us to enter into our inner world of intense feelings and emotions, shock and trauma, fears and insecurities. We are challenged to explore the meaning and purpose of our life after cancer. We are confronted with our sense of the sacred and of God. Walking through our inner world with gentle care is integral to our healing. Committing ourselves to this process eventually leads to a richer quality of life, characterized by an inner sense of well-being, a lived connection with ourselves, others, the sacred, God, and life. Failure to do so leaves us more or less limping through life, trying to move on from the trauma of cancer, bogged down by our unresolved cancer issues.

The challenge for many of us is learning to trust our inner experience, accepting that our feelings, fears, concerns and anxieties are all part of who we are. We tend to deny, rationalize, dismiss or minimize our inner stirrings. They seem unimportant as we try to survive the crisis and move on. Yet they tug at us, wanting to be listened to and respected. Healing from cancer requires that we take seriously what is moving within us.

The contents of this book have been alive within me for several years since my own cancer experience. For a long time, I gave myself multiple reasons and excuses for not engaging in this project---it would demand too much time and energy, and may never be published. However, the movement of my own spirit has been relentless in nagging me to write, to the point where it became imperative to give expression to what has been living in me for so long. And so, all these many years later, this book is born.

As a psychotherapist, spiritual director and energy healing practitioner, I tried to live through cancer with as much awareness as possible. Working with cancer patients and survivors in various contexts throughout the past several years has made me aware of the universality of the struggles, anxieties and fears experienced by those of us who have walked through cancer. This book is grounded in my passion to help guide patients and survivors through an inner journey that is crucial to moving on with our lives.

These chapters focus primarily on the first two years from the time of my diagnosis, which was a period of emotional and spiritual upheaval and turmoil. The last two chapters describe significant inner shifts that have occurred in my life as a result of having walked through the emotional and spiritual challenges of cancer. I have included excerpts from the journals I kept during that time, hoping that you, the reader, can identify with your own cancer story, and realize that whatever you have lived, or continue to live, is a normal part of the cancer experience.

As a way of guiding you through your own process, I have included questions at the end of each chapter for your reflection and journal writing. Reflecting on your personal journey can bring clarity to what you are living, facilitate your healing process, and help you move forward with your life.

May you feel supported as you read these pages. May they enlighten your own journey. May they help you realize that you are not alone. Whatever you are living today is integral to your healing.

I am grateful beyond words to my husband, Jeff, who has walked with me through all of it. His strong and faithful love has been constant as we together lived through my cancer experience. Throughout the many years of our marriage, he has always been there, supporting me in my many "out of the box" ventures, including the writing of this book. He continues to be my greatest cheerleader. In 2011, he himself was diagnosed with bladder cancer, which threw us once again into the shocking, uncertain and tumultuous world of cancer. Once more, our lives were turned upside-down. Today, as cancer-free survivors, we live grateful for being alive and healthy---with the unique distinction of being a cancer-surviving couple, something we certainly never sought!

My heart is filled with gratitude for my supportive family, siblings and their spouses, nieces and nephews and their spouses, for being there in so many caring ways throughout my ordeal, and for their untiring love and concern over the years. I cherish and treasure my family relationships. I love you all.

I am deeply appreciative for the care and love of my close friends, Sister Mary Anne Foster SC, Karen Laroche and Marie Evans who continue to be there as companions along this journey called life. I am grateful for the depth of our sharing and the enrichment I derive from these life-giving relationships.

Throughout my adult life, I have been blessed with a number of significant mentors and guides. Their support, guidance and challenge of many years ago have contributed immensely to my personal growth and deepening, which allowed me to live through cancer with reflective awareness. Their teachings continue to have a formative influence on my life. I am grateful to the faculty of the Institute of Formative Spirituality: Father Adrian van Kaam, CSSp, Ph.D. and Dr. Charles Maes, both deceased, Dr. Susan Muto and Dr. Carolyn Gratton. For many years, I worked with Dr. Vincent Bilotta, a good friend and colleague. Together, we developed and facilitated a number of innovative programs designed to help individuals discover and come home to themselves. Our work has enriched me both personally and professionally. I am also deeply grateful to Dr. Leslie Case, and Maurice Proulx, who, at different times in my life, each accompanied me through difficult challenges.

The gentle guidance of my Spiritual Director, Father Norman Comtois, OMI, continues to be a gift in my life. Our conversations have opened up profound places within my soul, that allow me to connect ever more deeply with the mystery of Divine Presence in my life.

I am indebted to my oncology specialists, Dr. Charles Simone, Dr. Arnold Herman and Dr.Edward Wittels for their professional expertise, and their willingness to take the time to engage my many questions and concerns. I continue to be touched by their compassionate care and understanding.

I gratefully acknowledge Dr. Sue Corrigan, Reiki Master and Shaman, for her invaluable help and support through the time of my diagnosis and first years of my healing process. I thank the members of Reiki Circle for their supportive presence and healing energy work through that time.

Throughout the past several years, I have had the privilege of working with a number of cancer patients and survivors in my private practice, through my volunteer Reiki work at local out-patient treatment centers, and with participants in cancer survivor retreats and workshops that I continue to facilitate. Their resilient spirit and desire to live a full life continue to be an inspiration to me.

A special note of gratitude to Jeff, Karen Laroche and Sister Mary Anne Foster SC for the time and energy each of them put into reading and discussing the first draft of this book. Their feed-back and comments have been invaluable in making these pages richer and more complete.

The team at Balboa Press has been extremely helpful, patiently guiding me through every step of the publishing process. I have greatly appreciated the expertise of Virginia Morrel, Barbara Carter, the Content Review team, and others who have contributed to the coming-into-being of this book. They have been wonderful to work with!

CHAPTER ONE

ENTERING THE WORLD OF CANCER

On November 23, two days before Thanksgiving, 2004, I received a call from the office of my primary care doctor for the results of a biopsy that had been done several days before. The medical assistant told me it would be good if my husband could be with me. "Was it bad news," I asked. "The doctor will tell you," was her reply. Suddenly, I felt limp. Why would she suggest that Jeff be with me unless there was a problem? Somewhere inside, I knew the news would not be good. I remembered that after the needle biopsy, I was given the name of a breast cancer surgeon. Dr. Livingstone, who had performed the procedure said, "You might need this." At the time, I was so frightened that I did not have the courage to ask her if I had cancer. I couldn't deal with it. Obviously, she knew the truth.

"The tests indicate that the lumps on your breast are cancer." The words "lumps" and "cancer" sank into my gut, making me sick to my stomach, as my husband and I listened to my doctor. In an instant, images of my Mother and two of my sisters, all deceased from cancer, flashed before me. Breast cancer, pancreatic cancer, ovarian cancer—and here I was with breast cancer. Their pain, their struggle, their debilitation and ultimate passing were in my face. I cried. Was I next? My family history taught me that women didn't survive cancer. The time between their diagnosis and death was painful, horrible and cruel. Was I headed for a similar fate? My doctor explained that the sonogram-needle-biopsy had revealed two cancerous lumps in my right breast. They had to be removed. Before we left her office, she gave me the name of a surgeon and scheduled an appointment. I was grateful that she had arranged and scheduled my next step. I felt numb as we left her office. It all felt surreal. "This couldn't be happening. I really didn't hear this."

My husband and I had driven to the doctor's office in separate cars, each of us coming from work. My body felt limp. I struggled to concentrate as I drove home in rush hour traffic. I couldn't think. I don't know how either of us got home, but we did. Everything around me was the same, yet different. In an instant, my life and world had changed dramatically. I was physically and emotionally drained. I couldn't make sense of the fact that I was walking around with cancer, yet feeling fine. How could this be? My husband and I held each other and sobbed. We had no words for what we were living--there were no words! Suddenly, our lives were changed---the ordinariness of our everyday life had been shattered. We had no idea, when we each left for work that morning, what the day would bring. I had been thrust into another world---a horrible world fraught with uncertainty and unpredictability. I was living a nightmare!

Throughout the weeks that followed, I walked around in the daze, while I continued to carry on in a business-as-usual manner. I felt split between my professional self that kept going, and my inner self that was in turmoil. In my attempt to maintain some sense of normalcy, I pushed aside my inner anguish and focused on my professional responsibilities. However, every now and again, those intense feelings broke through. I felt emotionally drained and exhausted. I sometimes wondered how I would make it through the day. Somehow, my inner strength carried me through.

My primary care physician had scheduled my next appointment with a woman surgeon. Surely, I thought, she would understand.

When we arrived at her office, we gave the X-rays and pathology reports to the assistant at the desk, who passed them on to the surgeon. She reviewed them in the privacy of her office, while we sat in the examining room, anxiously wondering what was going to happen. After a brief hello, and without examining me, she stated that "multiple sites on the same breast require a mastectomy." I couldn't believe what I was hearing. It was all too much to take in! She could do the surgery the following week. I was to have blood work done at the lab before I left, and would be contacted for a pre-op appointment. I was to call her within a couple of days to let her know what I had decided. She would then schedule the surgery. With that, she left the room. I sat there speechless, my head spinning.

We left her office stunned. As we sat in our car, I sobbed. My husband held me. "I can't do this." I blurted between my tears. "It's all too fast. A mastectomy!" I couldn't wrap my head around it. The possibility of losing a breast had not occurred to me. It felt too extreme! I wanted the cancer gone, but this was all happening too quickly! I needed to catch my breath. I needed to let it all settle--no way could I even think of the possibility of surgery the following week!

Thus began my journey into listening to and trusting my inner truth in regard to living this process. Where do I go from here? How do I navigate this medical maze? How and where do I find a surgeon with whom I will be comfortable? I felt so small in face of a huge and sometimes impersonal medical system.

I called my sister Elaine and my niece Michelle, both nurses who knew a number of doctors. Both of them gave me the name of the same surgeon, Dr. Arnold Herman. While speaking about him, my niece added, "He's the best in the area. I've recommended a number of women to him." Hearing that eased my anxiety. Perhaps he could help me. I called his office to schedule an appointment

My husband and I walked into Dr. Arnold Herman's office, both feeling scared, and not knowing what to expect. Here we were in one more examining room, about to meet one more doctor. Dr. Herman walked in, X-rays in hand. He greeted us, listened and spoke to us. He was kind, compassionate, reassuring. Immediately, I knew we were in the right place. He put the X-rays up, noting that he was looking at them for the first time, as were we. He calmly walked us through what he saw on the X-rays, pointing out the two tumors. I was too anxious to see clearly what he was pointing to and explaining. He laid out our options: a mastectomy or an extensive lumpectomy that would remove both tumors, leaving my breast disfigured. He also spoke of chemotherapy and radiation after surgery. Before doing any surgery, he wanted me to have a breast MRI in order to get a full picture of what was going on in both breasts. He suggested that we go home, and think about whether or not we wanted to work with him. If so, we were to call him; he would schedule the MRI. I walked out of his office feeling I had found the doctor with whom I wanted to work. He listened. He took the necessary time to explain. He was thorough. He answered questions. He was kind and compassionate.

The breast MRI was scheduled for December 15—more anxious waiting! I found myself moving in and out of panic, incredible fear and deep sadness. I felt I had no control over what was happening. Through these interminable days and weeks, I argued with God. "I've lived my life trying as best I could to be faithful to your movement within me. I've done your work. I continue doing your work. What is this about? I'm stopped dead in my tracks. Why? Why this? I've had it with cancer! I've lived through enough of it in my family!"

The day after the MRI, Dr. Herman called me with the results: there was a third lump in my right breast, deeper and close to muscle and chest wall. There was a shadow on my left breast. He scheduled a sonogram-needle-biopsy to determine what this shadow was. Both Jeff and I were in a place where more bad news was not welcome. We felt even more terrified. More cancer??? It was more than we could deal with! Would I survive this? Although I was distraught, I felt grateful for having pursued the advice of both my sister and my niece. As painful as this was, I now had a complete picture of the extent of the cancer in my right breast.

The biopsy was scheduled for December 23. My days seemed filled with doctor appointments and various tests. This was a dramatic shift from my history of seeing my primary care physician once a year for an annual physical! Here I was, thrust into the unfamiliar world of cancer: tests, biopsies, blood work, X-rays, doctor appointments, and more. It seemed never-ending! What a way to live the holiday season! Christmas was the furthest thing from my mind!

Within days, I found myself in another sterile room for yet another procedure. "Would this ever end?" I thought. I had been in this same room for my first biopsy. It stirred my deepest fears about the possibility of more cancer. I was teary---and very frightened. The doctor performing the procedure let me talk and cry. As I drove home from this biopsy on a dark, rainy, cold December afternoon, I experienced an inner shift in regard to this trauma: an invitation to befriend my experience of cancer—allowing all of it to teach me and transform my life. I felt the presence of my Mother and my sisters Jeanne and Anne, reassuring me that "All is well." What I did with this inner experience would be up to me. I could either dismiss it or trust it. It brought me a sense of calm in the midst of my inner fears and turmoil. I knew in my heart that God was with me, that my husband and family were with me. Although I did not know what lay ahead, I knew that I would have the courage and strength to live whatever the future held.

On December 30, we found ourselves back in Dr. Herman's office for the biopsy results. The good news was that my lymph nodes, lungs and liver were clear. But there was more. The biopsy revealed cancer in my left breast: a 1 cm. tumor with both ductal and invasive cells, and 1cm. of cancer around the tumor. It was time to look carefully at my entire situation and make the best decisions possible with the information we had.

Dr. Herman laid out the options for each breast. We asked many questions, which he answered thoroughly. His focus was on what I would be most comfortable with. What could I live with? He suggested that I call him the following Monday to let him know what we had decided. As Jeff and I discussed it over the next few days, I felt confirmed in what we had discussed with Dr. Herman: a right breast mastectomy and a left breast lumpectomy. Although I did not want a mastectomy, it became clear that it was indeed the best option, given the extent of the cancer in my right breast. The painful reality of what this meant sank in very gradually.

Needless to say, we went through the motions of the holidays. I had told my siblings about my cancer diagnosis on Thanksgiving Day. I was so grateful for a loving and supportive family as we gathered to celebrate Thanksgiving. My then 11 year old, usually quiet nephew, Stephen, took me aside, "Auntie, they're going to take the cancer out and you'll be OK" His words came from his loving heart into mine. I was deeply touched by his concern!

The days between Thanksgiving and Christmas were anything but celebratory. They were marked by doctor visits, tests and various appointments. In the midst of it all, I tried to maintain some sense of normalcy by continuing to work, knowing full well that my life was anything but normal. I was exhausted---and unaware that I was living in shock and trauma. I was simply going through the motions of my everyday life, more or less numbed out.

Throughout these difficult days, I found myself bouncing back and forth between my ego that wanted to know and control what was happening and my spirit that was aware that all of this was part of the mystery of my life. For my ego, keeping up my everyday routine was important. It provided a familiar structure, when everything else seemed out of control and somewhat unmanageable. Try as I may, I couldn't make sense of what was happening. Working and continuing to do what needed to be done at home gave me some sense of security and stability.

Spiritually, I felt grounded and centered. One day, as I walked through the house, I experienced a strong and clear sense that living through cancer was part of my spiritual journey. This experience made a powerful impression on me and stayed with me throughout the entire ordeal of surgery and beyond. I had known this to be true, that every life experience holds the potential for spiritual deepening. The clarity of this experience left no doubt. It carried me through my darkest times.

Christmas was fast approaching. I looked forward to our traditional Christmas gathering at our family homestead. No local family member misses this celebration. It's a wonderful time of reconnecting and celebrating. My siblings and their spouses, my nieces and nephews—all were there. All were very concerned. I felt the bond of caring love that had brought us together through the illness and death of four family members through the 90s. They were all there for me. I was not accustomed to being on the receiving end of so much love and care. As the oldest of a large family, I usually was there for others. Now it was my turn. I was being challenged to receive and allow myself to feel the depth of love from my family. I was challenged to ask for help—a very unfamiliar but comforting experience!

For many years, Jeff and I had a tradition of going out to a New Year's Eve dinner-dance. It was our way of remembering and celebrating what we had lived throughout the year, and blessing the year that lay before us. Neither of us was in a mood to celebrate. However, I was intent on honoring our tradition. "We are going out tonight. We'll enjoy ourselves and dance the night away," I said to Jeff. And so we did. For that night, we were able to put aside the trauma we were living. There would be plenty of time to deal with that later. Tonight, we stood at the cusp of one year that had brought us devastating news and the next that held so much unknown.

On January 3, 2005, we found ourselves once again in Dr. Herman's office to discuss the surgery. I told him that I had decided on a right breast mastectomy and a left breast lumpectomy, along with removal of the sentinel nodes. He affirmed my decision, telling me that under the circumstances, this was the best option. We asked questions about the surgery. It became more real as I left his office. I experienced a mix of feelings: scared, sad, strong, confused, anxious, not wanting to live this, hating it all…..and most of all, wondering if I would survive this ordeal. My family track record for surviving cancer was not encouraging. Thoughts of death were never far away. Would I too die like they did?

The surgery was scheduled for January 11. Pre-op testing on January 5 continued to make the reality of cancer more concrete. Yes, I did indeed have breast cancer. Yes, I had to have surgery. I could not escape what was happening. It was all very real---and very horrible! There was so much uncertainty. What would happen? Would Dr. Herman find more cancer as the surgery progressed? What did the future hold? So many questions. So much confusion. So little certainty! I felt so powerless. As difficult as it was, all I could do was live this process one day at a time. Those last pre-surgery days felt very long and somewhat unnerving.

Over the years, I had developed the ritual of taking a nightly bath. It was my time to be with myself, to soak in the tub, breathe deeply, sink into the warm, soothing water, and allow the day to wash over me. Throughout the weeks preceding surgery, I found myself caressing each breast gently and lovingly, doing Reiki on them. A few days before surgery, as I caressed my right breast, I sobbed deeply. "What happened to you? I've tried to take care of you. I don't understand. Why are you so filled with cancer? How did this happen?" Tears streamed down my face. Throughout most of my life, I had taken my breasts more or less for granted: they were simply part of my female body. Now, as I was about to lose one of them, they suddenly felt very precious. What would my body look like? How could I live with one breast? Deep sadness and fear overtook me. The night before the surgery, as I experienced intense emotional pain and terror, I tearfully said good-bye to my right breast.

For a few years, I had been part of a Reiki Circle, where a group of us, Reiki Practitioners and Reiki Masters, met regularly with Sue Corrigan, the Reiki Master Teacher who had trained us. It was a time for deepening our knowledge of Reiki and for practicing with each other under Sue's supervision. From the time of my diagnosis, I became the recipient of Reiki healing each time we met. Receiving Reiki brought me peace and calm. I also felt the support of the entire group. They all promised to send me Reiki on the day of my surgery. I was grateful for their work and support. Sue is also a Shaman. For several weeks before my surgery, she did Shamanic work with me. Both Reiki and Shamanic work brought a depth of inner peace that carried me through surgery.

January 11 finally arrived. We were to be at the hospital at 9am I woke up early, after a restless night. I got dressed and went out for a walk. I wanted to be outside---to feel the cold air against my face. I wanted to fill myself with the peace-filled stillness of nature all around me. I felt the need to walk to release tension and stress. I wanted to connect with God. The cold brisk air felt invigorating. The sun rose as I walked—the beginning of another day. For me, it was to be a day like no other. For the moment, however, I was content walking in the cold, welcoming the day—feeling restless, agitated and scared, as well as trusting that God would see me through this. The stillness and quiet of the early morning helped take the sharp edge off my inner turmoil. My strong relationship with God gave me the strength and courage to live this experience. I never wanted to have to deal with cancer. However, here I was, with no other choice than to face it and live it the best way I could. As much as I hated having to walk through this experience, I was aware of wanting to live it as consciously and clearly as possible. Life events and situations have the power to shape and mold us into the individuals we become. My desire was to grow emotionally and spiritually through this painfully difficult experience.

We arrived at the hospital. Jeff and I sat in the waiting area, holding hands tightly. We had been living with this reality for several weeks now. It had not gotten easier. I felt Jeff's love and support throughout all that had transpired. He was there for me in every way he could be. He too, was living this trauma. He feared losing me. I feared dying. Despite my own anxieties, I knew deep in my heart that I would be OK. Few words were spoken that morning. We knew what was in each other's heart. Our love for each other would carry us through this ordeal, as it had carried us through other difficult situations over the years.

Jeff and I had talked about what he would do that day. I had encouraged him to go to work. There was nothing he could do while I was in surgery, except to become more agitated and fearful. He left for work when I was called in. We hugged each other and parted, our hearts feeling full and heavy.

More pre-op work and procedures. Waiting to be brought from one place to another---all without being told what was next. I felt like an invalid, being moved around in a wheel chair. I wanted no part of it, but here I was. I felt numb in the bee hive of hospital activity. I was tired, hungry, terrified. I tried to just "be" but I couldn't. I closed my eyes on and off, wishing it would all go away. It was all a horrible nightmare---I would eventually wake up and life would go on. I tried to connect with myself; I felt agitated and could not settle down. I tried praying, but couldn't. I finally said, "God you know how terrified I am. Be with me. Help me."

Surgery had been scheduled for 2:30pm. I anxiously watched the clock. Minutes seemed like hours. I felt more and more tired, hungry and cold. 2:30 came and went. Still I waited. No one told me what was going on. Finally, after repeated questioning, I was told there was a back-up in the recovery room that created a back up in the operating room. Surgeries were delayed. I felt more frustrated and irritable. None of this eased my anxiety. By this time, I had a headache. I was restless. I wanted to get out of the wheel chair and walk around. I couldn't. I just wanted it all to be over!

Finally, at about 3:45, I was wheeled into pre-op and put on a stretcher. Dr. Herman came in to talk to me, to answer any final questions and concerns, and to reassure me that all would be well. Seeing him and feeling his compassionate care calmed me. I felt confident and secure in his hands. Over the days and weeks before surgery, I had prayed that Jesus would guide his hands through my surgery. As I was wheeled into the operating room, I had a sense of Divine Presence filling the room. That's the last thing I remember. I woke up in the recovery room with a painfully sore throat and feeling very groggy. The nurse wanted me to cough so she could remove the tube from my throat. In my half-awake-half-asleep state, I barely understood what she was telling me. I wanted her to leave me alone and let me sleep. I wasn't up for anything!

Eventually, I was taken to my room where Jeff was waiting. Seeing him was so reassuring! He stayed for a while, holding my hand. Dr. Herman had called him to let him know that the surgery had gone well. After some time, I asked him to leave. While his presence was soothing and comforting, I wanted to be alone. I was groggy and uncomfortable. I wanted to sleep.

It proved to be a very long night. Nurses were in and out of my room. Throughout the night, I dozed off, then woke up again, only to realize, as I looked at the clock on the wall, that it had been minutes. The night felt endless! I was restless. I could not sleep. I felt nauseous. I was miserable!

Finally, daylight broke through what had been a very long night. An aide brought in a tray with apple juice and jello. The sight of food made me more nauseous. I took a few sips of apple juice. I felt worse. I was hungry but couldn't eat. Jeff stopped by on his way to work. It was so good to see him! However, I felt so sick, that it didn't matter. The nurse injected anti-nausea medications into my IV, but that didn't help. Toward mid-morning, I asked for a real meal, thinking that might relieve my nausea----and it did. Gradually, I began to feel better.

Before surgery, I had heard that after a mastectomy, it is possible to develop stiffness in your arm, and lose flexibility, at least temporarily. Out of concern that that could happen, I began raising my arm as much as I could. What a relief to be able to raise it above my head! When Dr. Herman came in to check on me, the first thing I did was to raise my arm, feeling quite proud of myself. He smiled. He told me that the surgery had gone well. Now we had to wait for the pathology reports. After asking me how I felt, he decided that I should stay another night. I felt relieved---I wasn't ready to go home. I needed to catch my breath, and allow myself to sink into the reality of what had happened.

I slept on and off throughout the day. Physically, I was exhausted; I was uncomfortable. I had drains hanging from my incision. Layers of bandages covered my chest. Standing straight and moving around were a challenge. Emotionally, I felt numb. I was simply focused on getting well.

Jeff and some family members visited that evening. It was such a needed distraction. Soaking in their love and care was comforting. By the end of the day, I felt ready to go home the next morning.

I was discharged the next day, with instructions for home care. With Jeff, I was on my way back to the comfort of our home. I breathed a sigh of relief! I had survived the first step of what would be a lengthy process.

FOR YOUR REFLECTION
AND JOURNAL WRITING

1. Each of us carries within us our unique cancer story. Yet we all share some similarities. As you read this chapter, describe the connections you made with your own story.

2. Recall the day of your diagnosis. How did you react as you were told that you had cancer? What do you remember? Describe how you lived through that experience. What do you feel now, as you remember?

3. What stirs within you---thoughts, feelings, memories, insights---as you recall your experience of diagnosis?

4. A diagnosis of cancer requires having to make a number of decisions about surgery and treatment. Describe your decision-making process.

5. Allow yourself to breathe into whatever thoughts, feelings and memories you are experiencing. They are yours--to be handled gently and with care. Allow yourself to sink into what is stirring within you. Let yourself be with it all. Can you move gradually toward listening to, honoring and accepting your thoughts, feelings and memories as part of your story?

6. Sharing our story fosters emotional healing. It might be helpful to share your story with someone you trust, someone who will listen with care and compassion.

CHAPTER TWO

DECISIONS....DECISIONS....
AND MORE

I was back in the comfort and warmth of my home. Here, I could rest, relax and recuperate at my pace. My first challenge was attempting to get into bed. I soon discovered that I could not lie down--too much pain and discomfort. For several nights, I slept on the recliner---becoming quickly aware that I had to pay attention to what I was experiencing in my body. It was clear that I could not push myself.

Throughout those first several days, Jeff was there for whatever I needed. I felt safe and secure having him home. His loving care was such a blessing. However, I felt his fear and anxiety as well as my own. Every now and again, we shared what we were living around my having cancer. However, in my attempt not to add to his high anxiety, I found myself holding back, sharing only as much as I thought he could handle. I felt the need to protect him from the intensity of my thoughts and feelings. I was consumed with thoughts such as, "What will happen to me? I was cancer free now---for how long?" "What did the future hold for me---for us?" I was so frightened! Cancer meant pain, endless treatment, constant medical visits and procedures, diminishing quality of life, financial stress, and ultimately a cruel death by inches. I had seen too much of it in my own family.

My sister Jeanne had been diagnosed with breast cancer at age 40. For eight years after surgery, she was in and out of chemotherapy and radiation treatments followed by remission. She fought to live. However, her quality of life gradually diminished as cancer ravaged her body. At age 48 she lost her fight. It had been all so painful for our entire family! I was flooded with memories. Would the same happen to me?

Three months after my sister passed, Mom was diagnosed with pancreatic cancer---a crushing blow! I remember Mom saying, "You kids haven't gotten over Jeanne's death and now this is happening." So much pain! So much loss! Seeing Mom struggle, weaken and decline quite rapidly was heart-breaking. She passed five months after her diagnosis.

Six years later, my then 35 year old sister, Anne, was diagnosed with an aggressive form of ovarian cancer. Strong chemotherapy did nothing to stop the rapid spread of her disease. She passed six months after diagnosis. I was devastated! It seemed that the women in my family were destined to die of cancer. I was overwhelmed by all that we had lived as a family within a few short years.

The deaths and losses of those I loved had been extremely painful and heart-breaking. Through the years, thoughts of Mom, Dad, Jeanne and Anne were never far away. Jeff and I had lived through all of it together. We wondered whether I was about to walk a similar path. Yet, every now and again, since the time of my diagnosis, I sensed them with me, assuring me that all would be well. Trusting those words was a challenge as I lived my own process.

Cancer had turned my life upside down. It seemed that nothing was the same---and would never be. I led a busy life, as a self-employed psychotherapist, spiritual director and energy healing practitioner. My life had come to a screeching halt. It seemed that everything was on hold. Here I was feeling weak and vulnerable, dealing with pain, concerned about my future...wondering if I had a future!

Various angels filled my life throughout those first weeks of my recuperation. Family members and close friends stopped by, often bringing already cooked meals, which were such a gift. I received many encouraging cards and notes, which I read over and over---such a source of comfort! I felt supported by numerous phone calls from family and friends. In the midst of so many fears and uncertainties, I was so grateful for so much loving support.

Each day I felt stronger. My days were filled with doing arm strengthening exercises to minimize the possibility of lymphedema. I prayed and meditated. I read. Through it all, my spirit felt strong and alive. I had an inner sense that I would move through this alive and well.

On January 19, we saw Dr. Herman for my post-op visit. He reviewed the pathology reports, telling us that everything looked good. I had a mix of ductal and invasive tumors, and stage two and three cancer. While I heard every word he spoke, I was somewhat numb. He then raised the issue of chemotherapy and radiation. I shut down. I felt such an aversion to chemotherapy treatments! I had seen my sisters go through extensive and intense chemo, only to lose their quality of life, and eventually their life. I wanted no part of any of it!

I wondered about my next step. If not chemotherapy, what? What was the right path for me? What could I live with? While I was terrified of a recurrence, I was not willing to fill my body with toxic chemicals. There had to be another way.

As I prayed the following day, *"I had a moment of very strong clarity---focus on strengthening my immune system." (Journal, January 20, 2005)* But how to do this? I was not a medical person, nor did I know my way around the system. As my desire to strengthen my immune system grew within me, I wrote a long letter to Dr. Herman, expressing my thoughts about all of this. He passed it on to the oncologist to whom he was referring me.

I had also begun reading books on breast cancer and breast cancer treatment. Over the course of the next year and a half, I would read about twenty-five books. Each author had their own approach, depending on their particular experience and research. Most talked about nutrition, supplements, active life style. At times, the information was contradictory and confusing. At times, I felt overwhelmed---so much information, so many "do's and don'ts" about how to stay healthy after cancer. I was so frightened of a recurrence that I wanted to try everything that was recommended. I quickly realized that doing so was impossible. I had to find my own way through this maze of information, focusing on what felt right for me.

On February 8, Jeff and I met with the oncologist Dr. Herman had recommended. She went through all the details of my surgery, my cancer, and proposed treatment. She cited clinical statistics and percentages about treatment choices related to my specific pathology report. She spoke about my needing six chemotherapy treatments to kill any remaining cancer cells. I would also need radiation. I found myself inwardly resisting what she was saying. I knew chemo kills not only cancer cells, but healthy cells as well. My goal was to stay as healthy as possible for as long as possible. For me, chemo was not an option. Still feeling uncertain about asserting myself with expert medical professionals, I told her I would think about it for further discussion at my next visit. I left feeling both clear about what I wanted and confused with many "What ifs....." related to not doing chemo.

It was indeed a confusing time. Jeff is a Medical Support Assistant at the Veterans Administration Hospital in Providence, RI. Often, he came home from work sharing co-workers' opinions. "How can your wife even think of not doing chemo? She won't survive without chemo." These and similar comments left him even more concerned and frightened. I myself went back and forth--one minute thinking I should do chemo, and the next, trusting my deep inner sense that I wanted to focus on strengthening my immune system. During this time, Sue was very helpful. She did considerable one-on-one work with me. In the midst of my fear and confusion, she helped guide me back to my inner self asking me what I really wanted. In my deepest self, I was clear. However, when I focused on the standard treatment for breast cancer which is chemo and radiation, I became confused all over again.

After my medical appointments, my husband and I often had dinner at a local restaurant. During these months before and after surgery, this became a source of comfort. It also gave us the opportunity to process what we had heard. One afternoon as we entered the restaurant, I met an old friend. In our brief exchange, after I told her what I was dealing with, she shared her own journey: several years earlier, she too had had breast cancer, followed by chemotherapy and radiation. She was now dealing with serious heart problems as a result of treatment. This only added to my determination to explore other forms of treatment.

Thus began my online search for "what was out there." Eventually, I came across and bought <u>An Alternative Medicine Definitive Guide to Cancer</u>. (W.John Diamond, M.D, and W. Lee Cowden, M.D., with Burton Goldberg) This book described the approach to treating cancer of twenty-three physicians throughout the country. I wondered whether anyone could help me---so much information, so many varied approaches. How would I find the right doctor? How would I know which one was best for me? Would any of them be helpful? Distance, as well as their approach, would be determining factors. I read through the pages of this lengthy book, praying for guidance in choosing a doctor. This time-consuming process eventually led me to choose Dr. Charles Simone, M.MS., M.D., in Lawrenceville, NJ. I was attracted to his common sense approach to treating cancer.

> Dr. Simone is convinced that proper nutrition,
> nutrient supplementation and lifestyle modification
> help protect a person from developing cancer and

can be used as an adjunct to conventional therapies. The majority of his practice since 1982 has been with patients who have breast cancer or benign breast disease, and those who want to prevent both. The ultimate goal of Dr. Simone's approach is to win the war on cancer through prevention, early detection, and treatment "in which all options are fully explored," says Dr. Simone. (p. 394)

In a subsequent phone conversation with Dr. Simone, I felt reassured by his description of his approach to treating cancer. I was comfortable with his answers to my questions. However, I continued to go back and forth about going all the way to New Jersey to meet with yet another doctor. Would he even be able to help me? What was moving me to go so far? Why couldn't I just be satisfied with a local oncologist? There were certainly many of them in the area. This wasn't like me; I had generally gone along with and accepted what was. Why was I so intent on doing this? As I slowly began to distance myself from this inner conflict, I realized that I was fighting for my life and my quality of life. In the midst of this exhausting mental arguing, I continually returned to my inner truth: "Meeting with Dr. Simone feels right. What he's offering fits with my desire to strengthen my immune system as a way of fighting cancer." Although Jeff didn't understand fully why I had to do this, he supported my decision.

On March 10, 2005, barely two months after surgery, Jeff and I drove from Attleboro, MA to Lawrenceville, NJ, with all my pathology reports. I got very little sleep that night, feeling nervous about seeing yet another doctor. Would he be able to help me? What did he have to offer? Would I end up having to do chemo anyway? My questions were put to rest when we met with Dr. Simone the next morning.

This was the beginning of a long relationship that continues to this day. We walked into his office, not knowing what to expect, but feeling welcomed. Here was a doctor who, over the years, had treated prominent people such as Hubert Humphrey and Ronald Reagan. And here I was, an ordinary person seeking his help, wondering about the outcome of our visit. I immediately felt at ease with his kind, gentle, compassionate and unassuming manner. He listened to my story. He gave me a thorough exam. He reviewed my pathology reports. He then spoke to both of us, telling me that because I was post-menopausal and had estrogen positive tumors, I did not need chemo. I did need radiation and I had to be on Tamoxifen for five years. He explained why both of these were necessary. He then described his approach to treating cancer. He explained that three major factors contribute to most cancers: (1) nutrition, specifically a high fat, high cholesterol, high sugar and low fiber diet; (2) lifestyle; (3) environment. The inner environment of my body had been compromised, becoming cancer-friendly, he said. In order to minimize the possibility of a recurrence, the inner environment of my body had to be changed.

Dr. Simone then took us through the detail of each of the steps of his Ten Point Plan to prevent cancer and recurrence: (1) nutrition; (2) tobacco; (3) alcohol and caffeine; (4) radiation; (5) environment; (6) sexual-social factors, hormones, drugs; (7) attention to the seven warning signs of cancer; (8) stress modification; (9) spirituality, sexuality; (10) comprehensive physical exam. (Each of these is described in detail in The Truth About Breast Health - Breast Cancer, and Cancer and Nutrition, both by Dr. Charles B. Simone M.D.) He then suggested that I take the nutritional supplements he had developed over the years of treating cancer. These, he said, would reduce the risk of recurrence. He spoke about the importance of proper formulation of nutritional supplements as consisting of the correct nutrients, in the correct dose and correct chemical form, in proper ratio to one another. I began taking these supplements after that visit, and continue to do so today.

During our lengthy and thorough visit with Dr. Simone, I felt as though I were his only patient. My husband and I asked many questions. He walked me through a common sense way of regaining my health and staying healthy. I was impressed by his breadth of knowledge and experience. As we left his office, I leaned against the corridor wall and began to shed tears of relief! My body began to relax. Finally I had found a doctor who focused on strengthening my immune system. I felt comfortable with his suggestions. Over the years since that first visit, we have continued to see Dr. Simone twice a year in the beginning, gradually reducing our visits to once a year.

Two weeks after our return from NJ, I saw Dr. Herman, and shared my visit with Dr. Simone. Although he was a bit skeptical, he respected and supported my choices. When I expressed my dissatisfaction with the oncologist to whom he had initially referred me, he recommended Dr. Edward Wittels. He also referred me to a radiation oncologist.

On March 31, I met with my local oncologist, Dr. Edward Wittels. I found myself in another doctor's office in another examining room. Would this ever end? By this time, I was weary of doctors, medical buildings and examining rooms. I was also anxious. What would he think of my having consulted an out-of-state oncologist? Where did he stand in regard to chemo and radiation? Would I be able to relate to him? I met a kind and gentle man. He was easy to speak to. He was a knowledgeable and experienced oncologist. He listened as I shared what I had lived throughout the past few months. He reviewed my pathology reports, and spoke about chemo and radiation. I told him about Dr. Simone's recommendation. We discussed the issue of chemo. He gave me statistical information about patients with estrogen positive tumors who undergo chemo and those who don't. There was so little difference in the survival rate, that I felt confirmed in my decision not to do chemo. He respected my decision. I felt a good connection with him. He remains my oncologist today.

It is vitally important to be comfortable with our doctors. Being listened to and respected, being able to engage in conversation and ask questions, being confident that our oncologist is knowledgeable about the type of cancer we have---all of these are crucial. It may take some time to find the doctors we can best work with. While most patients and survivors have high regard for their oncologist, some have shared that at some point, they had to change their doctor. For various reasons, they no longer had confidence in him/her. When we find ourselves wondering whether or not we should stay with a certain doctor or facility, it is important that we move within ourselves to listen to what is going on. As we pay attention to our inner experience and talk to trusted others, eventually we will know from within what is right for us. Only we can determine who we can best work with and what is most life-giving for us.

On March 30, I met with the radiation oncologist who explained the process. I would have 35 radiation treatments. The number of treatments surprised me. When I asked her why so many, she replied that this was the standard protocol. How would all of this radiation affect my body, I thought. Would I be like my friend who experienced serious health problems years later? How would my body tolerate so many treatments? So many questions and concerns swirled within me. Radiation was not what I wanted, but it had been recommended by my doctors.

Despite my inner resistance and lingering questions, I began treatment on April 20. After the fourth treatment, I began feeling sick---flu-like symptoms and extreme fatigue. With each treatment, I felt sicker and more exhausted. I began realizing that through these symptoms, my body was telling me something: "Enough already! I can't tolerate anymore of this." I had been told that these treatments had a cumulative effect of exhaustion---but I had had only four treatments before the symptoms began.

After my seventh treatment, I told the tech that I would not return. Standing up for what I knew was right for me was challenging. Would discontinuing the treatments lead to a recurrence? Was I setting myself up for more cancer? Was this a crazy thing to do? When I stepped back from the questions churning within me, and connected with my inner truth, I knew it was time to end treatment.

Within a day or two, I received a call from the treatment center telling me the radiation oncologist wanted to meet with me. I met with her a few days later and shared my experience. She suspected that I had caught a bug, that what I was feeling had nothing to do with treatment. In my heart of hearts, I knew differently. Who was I to stand up to a doctor? Certainly she had more experience in this area than I did. Although she strongly encouraged me to continue treatment, my body was screaming, "No!" I managed to stand firm in what was right for me, telling her that at this time, I was discontinuing treatment. I left, wondering where my strength had come from. As I walked to my car, the mental questioning resumed. Who was I to go against medical advice? Why was I doing this? I got into my car, took a few deep breaths, and gradually moved back to the center of my being, where I felt comfortable with my decision. I had had the courage to respect what was happening to me physically, to listen to my inner truth, and find my own way in regard to the standard protocol for treating my cancer.

In hindsight, I realized more clearly that a diagnosis of cancer shakes us to the core. Our focus becomes "getting through" surgery, treatment and whatever else is involved. We live the experience feeling terrified and anxious. We want it all to be over so we can resume our life. In this terrified, traumatized state, we are expected to make important decisions about surgery and treatment---when our decision-making ability is colored by confusion, terror and high anxiety. It becomes easy to go along with what the doctors say. After all, they are the experts. However, it is important that in this process, we do not lose ourselves. Dealing with cancer is wearing and exhausting. Our energy is depleted. Asking questions, exploring and researching options is taxing and can seem overwhelming. Often, we cannot think clearly enough to ask questions. Having been thrust unexpectedly into the world of cancer, we may not know what questions to ask.

Each of us lives our journey through cancer in our unique way. I did not know ahead of time that I would make the decisions I made.

I listened to my doctors. I asked questions. I read. I researched. Jeff and I discussed the information we had. I took time to reflect upon and process what I heard and read. I prayed for guidance. Then I trusted what emerged gradually within me---what felt right for me, despite confusion and more mental churning. Over time, I gained clarity and tried to honor it. It was a challenging and time consuming process. Often I was overwhelmed. I was never far away from emotional turmoil and anguish. Endless questions continued swirling within me. I found myself holding it all---the emotions, the questions, the truth of my deepest self. Through it all, I was fighting for my life. I am grateful that I could gradually find my way by honoring my "inner knowing"---which I believe to be God's movement within me. I am also grateful for having doctors I can work with and who respect who I am and what I want.

FOR YOUR REFLECTION AND JOURNAL WRITING

1. Describe what you remember about your own recuperative process from surgery and/or treatment. Describe how you dealt with your fears and anxieties. Did you find yourself holding back with family and friends, concerned about not upsetting them?

2. Describe what spoke to you about your own decision-making process as you read this chapter.

3. Looking back to this decision-making time, are you comfortable with the decisions you made about treatment?

4. Describe your treatment process. How did you live it? What were your physical reactions to treatment? How did treatment affect you emotionally?

5. In the midst of the shock and trauma surrounding your cancer diagnosis, could you listen to your inner sense of what felt right for you? Describe any struggles you experienced in this process.

CHAPTER 3

STRUGGLING TO MOVE ON

I had had a right breast mastectomy and a left breast lumpectomy. I had come home from the hospital with my entire chest bandaged. When I saw Dr. Herman for my post-op visit on January 19, he removed the drains, then re-bandaged the area. I was to remove the bandages a few days later. That happened on January 22. Although I wanted the bandages removed, I did not relish the thought of seeing my bare and scarred chest.

Sue visited that day. Since she is a nurse, I asked her to remove the bandages. As she began the process, I became dizzy and felt faint at seeing the surgery site for the first time---I had no right breast! The area was swollen. A long scar crossed the right side of my chest. This was more than I could take! She slowed down the process so I could slowly absorb what I was seeing. I felt numb. Not wanting to undergo more surgery than necessary, I had decided against breast reconstruction. I had also spoken to women who had had reconstruction. Listening to them had convinced me that this was not something I wanted. Here I was, facing the consequences of my choice. I was shocked!

Later that day, I took my first bath since my surgery. I soaked in the tub sobbing as I looked down at my chest. My body would never be the same again. For days, I was teary on and off as the reality sank in---I truly had had breast cancer. My breast was gone---forever. For several months, I felt like a freak whenever I looked at my chest. I was damaged goods, never to be whole again. How could Jeff even look at me? He was gentle and understanding, yet for a long time, he was afraid to touch me.

Once the swelling went down, I was fitted for a prosthesis. I "looked" normal; however, every morning and night, as I dressed and undressed, I faced what had happened. Every now and again, I would choose not to wear my prosthesis as a way of moving toward accepting the fact that I had indeed lost a breast to cancer. It was a long, slow process. Yet, I have never regretted my decision not to have reconstructive surgery. I believe that my choice helped me face my reality. Slowly, over the next several months, I moved through and beyond the trauma of losing a breast to a place of acceptance.

My professional career spanned more than 40 years. I had worked successfully at a treatment center. I had been part of the founding vision of a sabbatical program, where I worked for ten years until a fire destroyed the building that housed the program. Since 2000, I have worked in private practice in Lincoln, RI. My work has been and continues to be life-giving and fulfilling. Although I knew I had to take time off to recuperate from surgery, it presented a bit of a challenge: this was the first time in my career that I was away from work for a number of weeks. For the first weeks, I had no desire to do anything, least of all meet with clients. Occasionally, I had thoughts of not returning to my practice. Perhaps it was time to retire. However, after a month, I gradually felt a desire to return to work.

Five weeks after surgery, I resumed seeing clients. I was also assisting Sue on numerous week-end workshops, which were always long and intense. Throughout my recuperation, I had been eager to get back to my "normal" life. Work provided that normalcy. Externally, I was moving full steam ahead, looking and feeling well. Internally, I was a mess.

I feel very sad about what has happened to me--breast cancer, mastectomy---and all that this means for the rest of my life---living in fear that it will return. I keep trying to pull myself up out of my incredibly deep sadness, skip over it so I don't have to feel it. The pulling up has exhausted me. I've been so tired all week. I find myself resisting sinking into it and allowing myself to BE in and with it. (Journal, May 21, 2005)

Throughout this time, I continued meeting with Sue regularly for Reiki and Shamanic work. Most of my session time was spent sobbing uncontrollably with unbelievably deep grief. My inner life was not in harmony with my outer life, which seemed to be moving along well. However, I could not escape the incredible fatigue I was experiencing. I was always exhausted. I had no energy, but I kept going. While I wanted time to simply hang loose, to put aside any responsibility for a while, all I knew was to continue moving ahead:

For the past two to three weeks, I've been experiencing a depth of soul weariness that I've not felt before. It's been there, along with a sense of "I've really lived through all of this. This experience of cancer has really happened to me"---the reality of it sinking deeper and deeper into my soul. Five and a half months after surgery, it's still hitting me more deeply---and I've felt so soul-weary! I've wanted to get away from everything---any kind of responsibility---for a while. (Journal, July 8, 2005)

Sinking into the harsh reality that I had lived through breast cancer was difficult to accept. I struggled to wrap my head around it! At times, it still felt surreal. The only way I could deal with it was to keep going. And keep going, I did! I went to work. I ran the house.

I engaged in social conversation and get-togethers. I saw and spoke to family members. Jeff and I kept busy on week-ends, engaging in enjoyable activities, especially as winter moved into spring and summer. I kept up the appearance that all was well and that I was moving on. However, within myself, I was living another reality. Everything and anything felt like too much. I felt heavy, tired, lost, empty. I did not know where to turn.

> *While I continue to feel deeply sad about what has happened to me, I'm experiencing a very deep and raw emptiness. The prominent image---a fallow field after the winter debris has been cleared and the field plowed, but not yet planted. Empty, waiting, recouping from the plowing process.*
>
> *I feel empty, lost. I don't know what I want. I don't want to do anything. I've lost my spark, my passion, my excitement about my work and about life. My life has been turned upside-down. I feel as though I'm starting over---with no clear direction. I do not see clearly. (Journal, May 26, 2005)*

Throughout the many years of my professional life, I had encouraged clients and spiritual directees to listen to and honor their experience. For years, I had taught and lectured about this--listening to oneself, and living in harmony with one's being. Throughout my life, I had grown into an attitude of listening to and honoring myself. I had navigated my way through surgery and treatment options by paying attention to what stirred within me. As I attempted to return to my "normal" life, listening to myself receded somewhat into the background. No matter what, I was intent on moving ahead in my familiar business-as-usual manner. Here I was, fighting my inner truth, choosing to push ahead, choosing to push aside what I was experiencing within the depths of my being. I felt that if I allowed myself to sink into what was going on within me, I would fall apart.

I would be unable to function. That was unacceptable. After all, I had many responsibilities. I had no choice but to keep going---or so I thought.

Eventually, my "running" caught up with me. I was always exhausted. I barely managed to get through the day. I was irritable and short-tempered. I felt like a porcupine with quills extended, ready to attack anyone who came too close---needing to protect myself from anything that felt like "too much." I had very little energy. I had lost my spark. The conflict between my inner and outer reality had reached its peak. I could no longer push aside my inner turmoil.

In August, 2005, I felt strongly that I needed time and space to BE with all that I had lived and was living. I made arrangements to spend a few days at a hermitage on the grounds of what was then Our Lady of Peace Retreat Center in Narragansett, RI, just blocks from Narragansett Bay. For as long as I can remember, I have been drawn to the ocean. The vastness of the sea expands my soul and spirit. I feel alive and free. I can spend hours sitting on a rock, soaking in the beauty around me, feeling connected with my deepest self.

My few days at the Hermitage were extremely healing---not without pain and struggle. I let my Journal do the talking.

On my first morning there, I wrote,

> *I woke up feeling so empty---a continuation of last night---no feeling, no images, nothing stirring---NOTHING AND NO-THING! Had a restless night. NOTHING, yet so much!*
>
> *As I was sipping tea just a while ago, I began to sob very deeply---with a parade of images of doctor visits--the moment I was told I had cancer; the moment Dr. Herman told me I needed a mastectomy; the moment Dr. Livingstone gave me the name of an oncologist and*

told me I might need to consult her at some point----I was too scared to ask her if she had found cancer; the moment Dr. Herman called me about more cancer, this time in my left breast, and more in my right breast; the moment before surgery when he came to check on me; the moment after surgery when I saw my chest covered with bandages; the moment Sue took off the bandages and I saw myself without a breast for the first time. It was all there, with such deep grief-filled screams. Sounds I haven't heard in myself ever---so very deep!

Seven months after surgery, such deep grief! As I sobbed I felt so deeply with each of these images, needing to get through the moment, the situation, the surgery, etc.---and in the midst of all this, not being in touch with or allowing myself to feel the depth and intensity of my own grief. Here it is, in my face!

As all of this has come up---the memories and the intensity of feeling---it's now very clear to me why I haven't been able to move forward---I've been carrying this intense grief and very deep sadness. It's still there; it's not over. (Journal, August 9, 2005)

While at the hermitage, I spent as much time as possible outside, feeling deeply connected with nature, going to the ocean, soaking in the sunshine and the refreshing sea air. I was up early in the morning, either sitting outside or walking to the beach, being part of dawn breaking into day. I did the same in the evening, experiencing daylight fading into dusk and darkness. I felt connected with this natural rhythm of dawn-daylight-dusk-darkness--living this same rhythm within myself.

I went down to the rocks this morning. I was grabbed by the ENERGY, PASSION, POWER,

31

> *FEARLESSNESS of the sea crashing on the rocks.*
> *It is endless---every moment of every day---crashing*
> *fiercely, gently, and everything in between, but*
> *always hitting the rocks. Changing the rocks slowly,*
> *imperceptibly over time, over days, months and years,*
> *transforming them bit by bit. Rocks changed forever by*
> *the action of the sea.*
>
> *I want for myself this kind of ENERGY, PASSION,*
> *POWER, FEARLESSNESS, as I live my life. I want*
> *to merge with the ENERGY, PASSION, POWER*
> *AND FEARLESSNESS of the sea. NOTHING*
> *stands in its way! NO-THING or NO ONE can stop*
> *it---ever! (Journal, August 9, 2005)*

That evening, I walked the half mile or so to the beach, filling myself with the expansiveness and aliveness of the sea. I walked the beach and eventually went for a swim, with the intention of cleansing myself of the pain, sadness and grief I was holding---it was freeing and exhilarating!

> *I feel free, cleansed and clear. My soul is in quiet*
> *stillness. I am at peace. I am no longer running. I've*
> *come home to myself, my heart, my soul! How good and*
> *wonderful it is to be home at last! (Journal, August*
> *9, 2005)*

The next morning:

> *I'm up before and with the birds, sitting outside in*
> *that mysterious time between darkness and daylight-*
> *--the earth filled with an eerie but soothing quiet*
> *and stillness. The birds just beginning to awaken and*
> *announce this new day.*

Today, this new day, symbolic of my own "new day." Newness within me. Pain, grief, loss, fear, lostness, anger have loosened their grip on me---no longer having power over me, no longer holding me back. They're still all there, but in their rightful place. So much coming up. I need to enter into the quiet stillness around me---and listen. BE STILL AND KNOW THAT I AM GOD! ENTER INTO THE STILLNESS....FEEL THE QUIET....BE.....

I feel one with the outer stillness that surrounds me. My soul is still---yet so much is surfacing! I feel the quiet of my soul, nourished by the quiet around me. Today...this new day---my new day. Being told strongly from within that I must write about my experience of cancer, focusing on finding one's way through the maze of treatment; standing up for what is right for me; the spiritual transformation of the experience of cancer. It's all so clear...and urgent. (Journal, August 10, 2005)

The process of allowing myself to walk through the pain I was experiencing led me to inner stillness and quiet.

The work of facing, owning, and beginning to deal with emotions holds the potential of allowing us to touch the depths of our being. For the most part, we resist walking through the feeling-and-working-through process. It is not fun! It is not easy! However, it remains essential to our healing.

Facing and allowing myself to feel my pain created space to take in the love and care I had experienced throughout the preceding months:

As I was walking back from the beach it began to rain---a soft, gentle summer rain---another cleansing, another washing away of pain, grief, loss, fear, doubt. The rain felt refreshing.

> *As I sipped tea, another video played inside me---moments of love and care throughout these months, especially around the time of diagnosis and surgery. Jeff's love, care and attentiveness---always there, always supportive no matter what; my siblings and my sisters-in-law---their keeping in touch, bringing food in the aftermath of surgery, expressing their love, care and concern--- respecting my choices even though they don't understand; Sue's continued care and guidance; Dr. Herman respecting my choices, trying to understand, telling me, "Claire, you will always push the envelope. It's up to us not to be threatened by you."; my neighborhood community---their care, visits, sending food; Reiki Circle ceremony before my surgery and their continuing to send Reiki during and after surgery; their continuing to keep in touch. Everything---all so powerful! Allowing myself to sink into the depths of all this care and love is challenging! I'm so accustomed to giving, not receiving! It's difficult to allow myself to take in the love, care and goodness that surround me. (Journal August 10, 2005)*

I felt new space within me. I held more than pain, sadness and grief. I could now feel and take in the love and care of so many significant people in my life. I "knew" they loved and cared for me; taking it in, allowing myself to sink into the depth of their goodness and kindness was a gift---a relief from what I had been dealing with.

I left the hermitage the next morning, grateful for having put aside this time to be with what I had been living for several months. It had been a rich healing experience. I knew I could no longer push aside the deep and strong emotions associated with my cancer experience. I became aware that facing and working through intense emotions is an integral part of dealing with cancer. I had been invited to integrate these emotions into the fullness of my life. I had to create the necessary time and space to listen to them, respect and honor them, live them in order to heal fully. Little did I know at the time, that I would be living an emotional roller coaster for the next two years or so.

For many years, I have had the privilege of accompanying cancer patients and survivors through their healing process. It has become clear that as we are living through the diagnostic and treatment process, we are simply intent on "getting through." Given the shock and trauma of the experience, we numb out, we push aside feelings, we do anything we have to do to "get through" in the best way we can. Our lives become a somewhat mechanical "getting to the next appointment, the next procedure, the next treatment." Once we find ourselves on the other side of it all, and begin to reenter the flow of everyday life, with its responsibilities and demands, the pain, sadness and grief begin to break through. Our reaction tends to be some version of, "Enough already! I just want to get on with my life. I don't have time to deal with these painful feelings." We tend to dismiss them and push them aside, as though dealing with them doesn't matter. Our culture tends to promote this attitude. We are encouraged to move ahead, to get things done, to produce, to get back into the swing of things as though nothing happened. Furthermore, we tend to pull ourselves up and out of our inner experience for the sake of our family and friends. It becomes important to "look good not to worry our loved ones."

Our emotions and feelings remind us that cancer touches more than our physical body. Physical healing from cancer is only part of our recovery process. Our emotional life needs time to heal as well. Allowing ourselves to sink into these painful places gradually leads us to more complete healing.

Our cancer story lives within us--- the doctor visits, waiting for and receiving tests results, determining the course of treatment, going through treatment---all of it lingers within us, inviting us to revisit it, the second time around, with greater awareness and with a willingness to own these experiences, gently and gradually, as an integral part of our story. Try as we may, we cannot deny the reality of what we have lived. It remains inscribed in our body and remembered by our body.

FOR YOUR REFLECTION
AND JOURNAL WRITING

1. Describe anything that touched your personal experience as you read this chapter.

2. Describe your process of moving back into the flow of your life---returning to "normal."

3. Describe your coping mechanisms---what you did to "keep going." Describe any dissonance you may have experienced between your "outer self" that perhaps looked well and your "inner self" that may have been in turmoil.

4. We deal with our emotions in a number of ways. We can listen to them and work with them. We can deny or rationalize them. We can push them aside as unimportant. We can ignore them and continue to push ahead. Describe your style of dealing with your emotions as you lived through cancer.

5. Could you allow yourself to grieve any changes in your body that resulted from surgery and/or treatment? Describe this process.

6. Our culture promotes independence and self-sufficiency. Describe your struggle to ask for help as you recovered. Could you receive and take in the love and care of family and friends? What was this like for you?

CHAPTER FOUR

RIDING THE WAVES
OF EMOTION

Although life went on, I felt very vulnerable. I felt I was walking on eggshells---tentative, uncertain, unsure of myself. Life felt unpredictable. I lived in fear of a recurrence. I became extremely attentive to what I ate, not wanting to put chemicals into my body, watching my fat and sugar intake, per Dr. Simone's suggestion. Much of what I was reading reinforced the Ten Point Program he had developed years earlier. Whenever I was out walking, I feared taking in car and truck fumes--I held my breath and covered my nose and mouth. I increased my exercise, working out almost every day. TV and newspaper reports related to cancer grabbed my attention, while also stirring fear in the pit of my stomach. I often felt on the verge of tears. I was living vigilant, guarded and apprehensive, doing whatever I could to remain healthy and prevent a recurrence. The stress of it all exhausted me.

Around the time of the one year anniversary of my diagnosis, I felt uneasy, uncomfortable, sad, hurt. I began to realize that I was living feelings I hadn't experienced at the time of my diagnosis. I was gradually coming out of the numbness of trauma and shock, thawing out, so to speak.

I feel weary, sad, tired. A couple of weeks ago, I felt heavy, very sad, exhausted, with a different quality to it. I didn't know why, until I realized that it was last Nov. 1 that I saw Dr. Alves for my annual physical---the day she found the lump on my right breast. Little did I know then what was to be set in motion! I found myself two weeks ago reliving the events of last year, with a depth of feeling I didn't and couldn't experience then. I was shocked and dazed---in survival mode, focusing on "getting through."

Since that day two weeks ago, I've been running, feeling the need to sit in quiet, feeling the need to write---and running. Afraid of the depth of feeling. Afraid of the pain. Afraid that if I sink into all of this, I won't be able to keep going as I have been. Too much hurt! Too much pain! (Journal, November 15, 2005)

These were difficult and challenging days and weeks. Although I was moving on the best I could, those feelings and emotions I had pushed aside unwittingly, remained alive in my body. My body remembered in ways my mind didn't. The good news was that I was thawing out from the numbness of shock and trauma. At this point, a year later, I had no idea that I was still numbed out. This anniversary time put me face to face with more raw emotion.

Reliving the trauma of last year---these days, these weeks. The shock of a cancer diagnosis---deep pain, sadness, grief, anger. And such deep gratitude that I am well! That there is no more cancer. It's all there, in my face! (Journal, November 27, 2005)

The first anniversary of my surgery led to reflection on what I had lived throughout the year:

At this time, a year ago today, I was in surgery for breast cancer. Today has been a very rich day! For the past two weeks, I've felt a depth of pain that made me feel I was going to die---loss; grief; the felt awareness that I lost a breast to cancer; recurrent fear and anxiety. I was simply going from one thing to the next, tears never far away! So many tears, so much sobbing, such deep wailing! So much deep and intense pain! So much anger and rage---Why cancer??? Why me??? I hate it. It's the dark, lost, awful space I've been in. A couple of days ago, from deep inside came, "You're alive and well! You need to celebrate." I felt like a ping-pong ball, bouncing from the pain of so many images and memories from last year---to feelings of being alive and healthy. Today, I celebrated, taking time for myself, which I don't often do. I went out to lunch. I bought some clothing. I bought myself a rose. I did moving meditation. All of this was pleasurable. I felt free. I experienced joy. I felt happy! WOW!!! (Journal, January 11, 2006)

As I have lived my own experience, and accompanied other cancer survivors, as well as clients and directees dealing with traumatizing events and life situations, I have become aware that the first year anniversary of the trauma awakens memories, emotions and feelings that they could not deal with at the time of the trauma. A serious health crisis such as cancer, the break-up of a marriage, the death of a significant other or family member, the loss of a home through fire, a financial crisis----these and more plunge us into "survivor mode." Feelings and emotions are repressed as a way of helping us survive and move through the trauma. We numb out emotionally. Repression is an automatic mechanism that protects us from becoming overwhelmed and unable to move through the traumatizing situation.

Repressed feelings however, do not disappear. They tend to emerge about a year after the traumatizing situation. Then we have a choice: we can either push them aside, which adds to our stress, exhaustion and depression, or we can do the hard and challenging work of facing them and working with them, which leads eventually to greater self-awareness, a sense of inner well-being and harmony, and a richer quality of life.

Throughout my adult life, I have been committed to self-awareness and personal deepening. Faced with the intensity of these "thawing out" feelings and emotions, I knew I had to walk through them. They were part of my life experience, part of who I was. I had no choice but to allow myself to plunge their depths. It was a difficult and challenging process that has gradually led me to a deeper connection with myself, with life, with God. I feel freer and more whole as a result of having walked this path.

The waves of deep emotion continued to come and go for what seemed like a long time. For about two years after my diagnosis, I felt little relief from the onslaught of intense emotion. I bounced back and forth between profound pain and deep gratitude for being alive and well.

During my daily two mile walks, I was often hit with intense fear and terror that cancer would return. My fear was alive and well in the pit of my stomach. My breathing became shallow. I became teary and often cried as I walked. I felt helpless and powerless. My body had turned against me; how could I be sure it wouldn't happen again? As I walked, I began to pray, "God, my life is in your hands." I repeated this over and over. For a long time, these words remained simply words---an intellectual concept. Over time, however, they became very real---they sank into my heart. I knew and felt from deep within, that my life was truly in God's hands. I felt I lived in partnership with God: I could only do my best to remain healthy; the rest was out of my control. As this truth took root in my heart, the intensity of my fear and terror gradually eased.

This is not to say that I no longer fear. Whenever I experience a new and different place of physical pain and discomfort, thoughts of possible cancer surface. However, these thoughts come and go. They no longer absorb my energy. I live from an inner knowing that my life truly is immersed in God.

This belief seemed to provide the inner security and courage I needed to face some of my strongest emotions. I found myself suddenly filled with anger, rage and hate about having to live through cancer. I had seen enough of it in my family throughout the 80s and 90s. I wanted to move on with my life. Cancer was a major disruption. I wanted no part of it! Living this was all too much!

> *I've felt drawn to doing some finger painting. It took some pushing myself to make myself do it. I just finished two paintings---one with my hands, the other with my feet. I felt rage and fury---the words, "It's been a hell of a year!"---deep crying and sobbing. I was able to admit to myself, "Yes, it has been a hell of a year. It's been hell!"*
>
> *I realized that whenever those feelings have come up, I've gone to the other side of gratitude for being alive and well. I've not allowed myself to sink into those painful hellish places. Going there, being in those places scares me. The depth of these places terrifies me. I don't want to be engulfed in the pain, the terror, the horror---and perhaps even the despair of it all. It's all too much! (Journal, February 2, 2006)*

My anger was also focused on the diagnostic process. For years, I had had an annual mammogram. My most recent had been done in April, 2004, seven months before my cancer diagnosis. I was filled with "Why?" "Why didn't this show up in my April mammogram?" "Why didn't they see it last year or the year before?" "Why didn't my doctor feel this lump before?" My anger intensified when both my surgeon and oncologist told me that this cancer had been growing in me for about three to five years. How had this been missed? When my surgeon scheduled me for a mammogram the year after surgery, I laughed cynically, saying, "A lot of good that will do!" I continue with my annual mammogram, aware that at this time, it is a good but imperfect diagnostic tool. However, a degree of skepticism remains with me.

Hate accompanied my intense anger. As hate filled me, I found myself spontaneously expressing my own litany of hate:

> *I hate having had to live the experience of cancer!*
> *I hate cancer!*
> *I hate having lost a breast!*
> *I hate that cancer has changed my life!*
> *I hate having to pay attention to myself---my energy level, my fatigue!*
> *I hate not having the energy I used to have!*
> *I hate not being able to push myself to do what I have to do!*
> *I hate having to restructure my life!*
> *I hate that I'm no longer in charge of my life!*
> *I'm angry and furious!!! I can't stand this! And deep inside, I hear, "Remember who you are. You are not your cancer or even your fury. You are Light. Embrace yourself as Light. You are not your energy level. You are light refined in pain and suffering--- made brighter, clearer, more vibrant. Believe in who you are." (Journal, February 27, 2006)*

Expressing and releasing these intense feelings was extremely draining. Doing this work exhausted me. As painful and unpleasant as it was, facing my feelings and emotions was a necessary part of my healing process. Eventually, fear, anger, hate, rage, loss and grief loosened their grip on me. I felt freer. As I plumbed the depths of my anger, fury and hate, I touched more deeply into my own spirit, that place of inner strength, courage, resiliency and light.

I am convinced that facing and walking through the strong emotions that accompany the cancer experience is essential to healing. As noted earlier, feelings and emotions do not go away. While we may be physically well, we cannot move on with life fully unless we allow ourselves to do the emotional healing required to live a richer and more satisfying life.

In June, 2006, a local hospital was offering a six-week transition group for cancer survivors who had completed treatment and were moving on with their lives. I felt drawn to participate in this group. I had been feeling alone throughout these long months of dealing with intense emotion. Yes, I was meeting with Sue regularly; however, I felt I needed more. As we went around the table introducing ourselves during the first meeting, I felt at home. I felt "normal." Each in our own way, the eight of us were describing similar experiences: we felt out of control; we experienced low energy; we wanted our old life back.

> *I feel raw, vulnerable---an open wound inside. First meeting of the transition group tonight. As we went around the room, introduced ourselves and told our stories, I found myself sinking into that part of my reality---I do want my old life back. I have no control. My life will never be what it was. I don't know where I'm going. My energy level has changed, etc....*
>
> *I felt in every cell of my body that I've tried to keep things as they were---participate in numerous week-end workshops with Sue; keep the house going; do everything that's expected of me---or that I expect of myself so that I feel "normal." For perhaps the first time since my cancer experience, I felt "normal" tonight, listening to other women share struggles similar to*

mine. I didn't have to pull up. I didn't have to be where I'm not.

It's all so subtle. Yet, I felt it so deeply tonight--- what I do to myself to convince myself that everything's OK. (Journal, June 5, 2006)

Participating in this group proved invaluable. I felt the support of other cancer survivors as we all struggled to move on. What became clear to me through these six weeks was that I would never get back my pre-cancer level of energy; that I had to pay attention to and respect my energy level; that I could not get my old life back; that moving forward from cancer meant making changes in my life. If I chose not to make these changes, I would remain stuck in the limbo of trying to recapture a life I could no longer have. My pre-cancer life was gone---forever!

During one meeting, we shared our fears about moving forward. None of us felt we had any control over our lives. All of us felt lost, with no sense of direction. The group facilitator commented that each of us had faced the possibility of death through cancer. Having faced death, she said, what more did we have to fear? Her statement stayed with me, and helped me move through my own fears. Yes, I had indeed faced the possibility of dying. I didn't know what the future held, but today I was healthy. "Today" is all I have.

FOR YOUR REFLECTION AND JOURNAL WRITING

1. Read through the following list of feelings and emotions slowly and reflectively. Which ones have been or are part of your cancer story? You may want to check those that are alive in you.

Sad	Numb	Hopeless
Angry	In shock	At peace
Confused	In denial	Weary
Anxious	Helpless	Calm
Powerless	Desperate	Exhausted
Beside myself	Debilitated	Devastated
Low energy	Out of control	In disbelief
Why?	Sick to my stomach	Traumatized
In crisis	Depressed	Can't cope
Afraid of dying	Why me?	Panicked
Where is God?	Frightened	Alone
Terrified	Angry at God	Courageous
Strong	Shattered	Discouraged
Like a zombie	In turmoil	Isolated
Crushed	Empowered	Emboldened
Distraught	Despondent	Grieving
Lost	Victimized	It's not fair
Empty	Can't think straight	Resilient
Determined to fight	A nightmare	This will kill me
No feeling	I can't do this	It's too much

My life is in an upheaval	This can't be true
I don't know where to turn	Surreal; this can't be happening
It'll all be gone when I wake up	My life is turned upside-down

45

Nothing makes sense anymore	I want my old life back
Walking around in the daze	Grateful the cancer was found
Grateful to be alive	Pulling myself up to get through
Keeping a stiff upper lip	I don't know where to turn
My life is over	The rug is pulled out from under me
Trusting I'll be OK	Relying on God
More appreciative of life	Overwhelmed by too many decisions
My life has deeper meaning	Awakened to the small things of life
Searching for myself	Who am I?
I don't know what I want	Unclear about where I'm going
I don't know who I am	I'll never get over this
Cancer will not control me	Finding a new direction
Surrender to God's will	Cancer has changed my life
Afraid of my feelings	Denying my feelings
Facing my feelings	I don't want this
Scared to death	I feel strong

Protecting others from my pain and fears
Holding in feelings not to upset family, spouse, co-workers, friends, etc.

2. Feelings are neither right nor wrong. Whatever you are experiencing is simply a reaction to living through the trauma of cancer. Honor and respect what is stirring within you. Note the feelings, emotions and phrases with which you can identify, without judging or blaming yourself.

3. Note those that awaken something in you or provoke a physical reaction, such as butterflies in your stomach; physical tightening; a sick-to-your-stomach feeling; a change in your breathing, a headache, restlessness, anxiety, resistance, tension, etc. Dwell with whatever is moving within you physically and/ or emotionally. Your reactions are an invitation to face and walk through your emotional experience.

4. You may want to journal with whatever you are experiencing as a result of reading through this list. Giving written expression to what you are living is a step toward self-awareness and inner freedom.

5. Where are you in the process of looking at, facing and working through your cancer-related feelings and emotions? Do you take them seriously? Are you afraid of them? Do you find yourself running from them? Can you walk through them, to a place of gradual acceptance?

CHAPTER FIVE

SHOCK....CRISIS....BLESSING

Receiving a cancer diagnosis was devastating---something I never expected. Despite my family history, I was not prepared for this. I had lived with cancer in my family of origin for many years. I now found myself living through the experience myself. I could see no further than what I had witnessed in my family. I too would die of cancer. For about eighteen months, I lived in shock, without realizing it.

Although I had resumed my everyday routine, I felt extremely vulnerable. I felt broken. After a support group session during which we worked with Play Doh, I wrote,

> *I'm holding the Play Doh piece that I made at last night's group---giving expression to fear, sadness, anger. I felt a very strong desire to shape it and poke holes all over it to represent my feeling broken. Holes have been poked in my familiar way of being and living---I can no longer go full speed ahead; I have no choice but to listen to my body, my energy.*
>
> *I can no longer be inconsistent about going for walks; I must do it to promote health.*
>
> *I can no longer eat anything I want. I have to stick to low-fat, low-sugar---this is challenging at times.*

Many of my old beliefs have crumbled. I don't even know which ones. I only know that they're gone. Everything feels different inside.

I've lost my enthusiasm and my passion. I don't know what I want. Sue suggested that I work with that. I'm just not there. I can't do it.

I feel lost, confused. I don't know what I want or where I'm going. I don't know who I am anymore.

I feel like Humpty Dumpty who fell off the wall and is in pieces. I don't know how to put the pieces back together again. The truth is, the pieces can't be put back together in the same way...... So frightening! So terrifying! But I also live each day with a deeper gratitude and love. Little things make me stand up and take notice. I truly am all over the place, bouncing from emotional pain to a spirit-awareness that there is more to my life than this crisis.

In the midst of all this, I feel clarity deep in my soul. Yet, it frightens me. The clarity is about moving ahead---moving forward, getting myself out there with what I know I'm called to do---work with women with cancer. In all my feeling lost and confused, this is the one piece of clarity! Putting myself out there scares me! As I hold my Play Doh, I feel myself sinking into depths of sadness and grief. A bottomless well! (Journal, June 13, 2006)

I felt a split between what I was experiencing emotionally, and what I sometimes sensed momentarily within the core of my being. An image that often came to me was that of the ocean during a severe storm. The surface of the ocean rages. The waves are swollen, furious, tumultuous and agitated. They crash relentlessly against rocks and retaining walls. But hundreds and thousands of feet below the surface, all is calm. There is not even a sense of the storm raging on the surface.

Often throughout those first two years after diagnosis, I lived primarily in the raging storm. Every now and again, I experienced brief moments of inner peace and clarity---a relief and respite in the midst of the storm's fury! I often wondered when the storm would end. When would I regain my inner peace and calm? When would I get my life back? When would things make sense again? How long?......

My cancer diagnosis has been the most challenging crisis I have faced in the course of my life. I knew, from so many other difficult life experiences, that I had a choice. A life crisis is like a fork in the road. We can either live it stuck in fear, anxiety, anger, bitterness and resentment, or we can see it as an opportunity for personal growth and deepening. For the most part, this choice is not clear as we live the crisis. We put all of our energy and effort into "getting through." We find ourselves living in survival mode, often without even being aware of it. Only as the shock begins to wear off, and as the frequency of treatment and medical appointments diminishes do we slowly realize that we do indeed have a choice.

A life crisis, such as cancer, holds the potential of leading us within and opening us to our inner depths. Living through the trauma and uncertainty of cancer led me into the depths of my spirit---into those inner resources that we're not usually aware of in our day-to-day living. At every step, I found myself looking within, focused on "What's right for me?" though it was often unclear and muddled. I stayed with the question until I felt that what was unfolding within me was an expression of my inner truth. I discussed every decision with Jeff, who feared that if I did not go along with traditional cancer treatment, I would eventually have a recurrence and die. His anxiety, coupled with my own, led me at times, to question my own choices. However, when I stepped away, inevitably, I returned to an inner sense of certainty about what was right for me.

I experienced a quality of strength and courage that I didn't know I had. I found myself speaking up to doctors about not wanting chemotherapy and radiation, while I trembled inside, wondering how they would react. I searched out an oncologist who integrated healthy life style and specific nutritional supplements in the treatment of his cancer patients. I had always considered doctors to be "the experts," and had never challenged their treatment decisions. Here I was, challenging, refusing to go along with an oncologist who insisted on chemo and radiation, and who, when I asked what I could do to strengthen my immune system, told me to eat more broccoli and cauliflower---which I had been doing for years.

That same strength and courage led me to dismiss the statement of another oncologist who maintained that nutrition and exercise played no part in living a healthy life-style after cancer. When I ended radiation after seven treatments, I argued back and forth within myself, wondering whether I would die if I didn't have thirty-five radiation treatments---or, if I had thirty-five treatments, would I die from the long-term side effects of radiation. While the doctor's comments led me to question my decision, I knew deep within myself that this is what I had to do. I was surprised by my ability to assert myself with medical professionals.

I discovered my inner resiliency, determination and tenacity as I walked through the long days and months of this ordeal. No matter how bad the news throughout the initial long weeks of diagnosis, no matter how deep my fear and anxiety, I eventually went to that inner place of picking myself up and living with the reality of my situation. Despite being unaware that I was in shock and trauma, I was determined to live through this experience as consciously aware as possible, to read all I could about breast cancer and treatment, and to try to make clear decisions. This proved to be a challenge; however, I strongly believed that no matter how difficult the situation, how frightened and anxious I felt, or how emotionally distraught I was, I had to be faithful to my inner truth. Whatever the long term outcome of my decisions, it was important to me that I remain faithful to the inner movement of my spirit.

As I moved away from the decision-making phase of my cancer experience, I found myself living with a greater appreciation for the gift of life, for the dawning of another day that was mine to live as fully as possible. As a result, life has taken on greater meaning and importance. Each day brings its challenges, its surprises, its unexpected moments, as so many invitations to learn and grow. As appreciation for each day has become a way of life, I have felt my spirit expand.

Throughout the years since my owns struggle with cancer, I have been privileged to work with a number of cancer patients and survivors in my private practice as well as in my volunteer Reiki work at local hospitals. I continue to be inspired by the strength, courage, resiliency and determination of these women and men. They talk about wanting to get better. At times, they share their fears and concerns. However they may be feeling physically, their spirit is alive and strong, even in their weakest moments.

Since my Master's work in Formative Spirituality at Duquesne University in the 70s, I have been committed to personal growth and spiritual development. I left the program aware that my life had been changed. If I was to work intimately with individuals as a spiritual director and retreat facilitator, it was important that I continue my own inner work. I was also aware that the ordinary "stuff" of everyday life, the persons, events, situations and things that constitute our life become so many invitations to grow in relationship with ourselves, others and God. I believe that every life experience becomes an opportunity for learning. Living through cancer, then, became an invitation to look at my life.

Having been trained in a variety of energy healing modalities, I found myself reflecting upon our female breasts from an energy perspective. As I began to sink into the reality of having lost a breast, and having had a lumpectomy in my second breast, I focused on the nurturing, nourishing quality of our female breasts. Women tend to be givers and nurturers, often putting aside our own needs, to care for others--spouse, children, family members, friends, neighbors, colleagues,---the list can become endless. We easily give to everyone but ourselves, often without a second thought. Honoring our inner truth, respecting our limits, paying attention to our fatigue, listening to our need to step back and take a few breaths, caring for ourselves, learning to say "no"---all can be challenging for most women. Most of us live with an imbalance between caring for others and caring for ourselves.

As I looked at my own life, it became clear that I had spent most of my life nurturing others as older sister, wife, teacher, spiritual director, psychotherapist and energy healing practitioner---and more. My life was about caring for others. I sometimes had glimpses of the imbalance between caring for others and caring for myself. While I did things to care for myself, I became aware that I was "doing-things-for-myself" rather than living from an inner attitude of caring for myself. It was primarily about "doing" without spending much time listening to my energy level, my needs, or the deep desires of my heart. I felt as though my breasts were telling me, "We've given so much, there's nothing left. This cancer is a wake-up call to change things, to live a more balanced life."

The Great Commandment that Jesus describes in the Gospels came alive in new ways. When asked which commandment was the greatest, Jesus replied, " 'You shall love the Lord your God with all your heart, and with all your soul, and with all your mind.' And a second is like it: 'You shall love your neighbor as yourself.' " (Mt. 22:36-39, as quoted from The New Revised Standard Version of the Bible) Over the years, I had heard these verses quoted frequently. I had often listened to homilies about "loving your neighbor." Rarely had I ever heard anyone talk about Jesus commanding us to love ourselves. As I recognized the imbalance in my life, I heard, "love your neighbor as yourself," quite differently. I began to focus on "love yourself". Jesus was telling me that it is just as important to love myself as it is to love others, that my care for others needs to be balanced by caring for myself. I could no longer continue to ignore my own needs. I had to pay attention to my energy level and my human limitations. I had to listen to my needs for rest and relaxation, for pleasure and peer connection. I had to honor the deep desires of my heart.

Developing a caring attitude toward myself has proven to be a challenge. I have had to face and deal with considerable guilt and feelings of being selfish intertwined with many "shoulds." Whenever I felt a need for a break, "I should keep going," reared its head. Whenever I felt the need for a nap, another voice made itself heard, "You're not supposed to take a nap. Just keep going." Often when I sat to read a book or went out for a walk, I was confronted with "You're wasting time." Whenever I bought something for myself or went out to lunch with a friend, I was assaulted with, "This is a waste of money. You shouldn't be doing this." Although these harsh voices have subsided as I have given myself permission to care for myself, their echo can be heard occasionally even after several years of paying attention to bringing more balance into my life. Those entrenched inner voices die hard!

Having worked with many women in psychotherapy and spiritual direction for many years, I have realized that caring for ourselves is a common struggle for most women. Yes, we are nurturers and caregivers. However, it is vital that our caring for others be balanced with a gentle and respectful self-care and self-nurturance. It is important that we not simply "do" self-caring activities, but that our self-care flow from an inner attitude of self-love and self-respect.

As a result of living through cancer, my sense of God has changed. God has always been an important part of my life. I was raised in a family where religion was important. Through my Catholic education and years in the convent, God had become real for me. During my Graduate Studies I was introduced to a spirituality grounded in who we are as unique individuals and in the reality of our ordinary life. I learned that spirituality is about growing in intimacy with God through the persons, events, situations and things of our everyday life. This was both freeing and challenging.

I was invited to grow in self-awareness and to pay attention to my everyday life experience as ways in which God is present in my life and invites me into an increasingly intimate relationship.

This approach to spirituality continues to guide and sustain me. As I was walking through my house shortly after I was diagnosed with cancer, I experienced a clear sense that living through cancer was part of my spiritual journey. I knew within the core of my being that living this experience had the potential of deepening my spiritual life and my relationship with God. Little did I know where it would lead me!

Throughout those first two years, I often wrestled with God. This was especially true as I realized that I could not go back to the way things had been:

> *I feel so raw--I want to roll up into a cocoon and protect myself. I could never have imagined the depths of emotional turmoil my experience of cancer would throw me into. "I want my old life back" is so strong with me. Equally strong is the awareness that that will never happen. God, where are you leading me? Leave me alone! Enough already! I can't take this. While I know and can state that it's about moving forward from here, everything inside me screams NO!--I want to go back to how things were. Ironically, I don't even remember how things were--what a waste of energy!*
>
> *Tuesday as I was sobbing, I felt, "I don't want to fight anymore! I don't want to fight your movement in my life, God."---and with that came deep and profound fear of the unknown of moving forward. I feel gripped by that fear. Yet, I want to surrender to God's ways for me. I want to let go of being in control---even though I'm not really in control of anything---a hard lesson learned from cancer! But I'm so scared of what it all means. So terrified of letting go!*

*I wrestle with myself. I wrestle with God. I'm
so tired and worn out by all the fighting, but I don't
know any other way. I feel I'm fighting for my life.
(Journal, March 2, 2006)*

And so it went for a long time, until I gradually surrendered
to the fact that my life indeed had changed, that I could no longer
return to the past, that I had to move forward. I slowly began to trust
God's movement in my life, as I had done in the past. Somehow all
of that had gotten lost as I lived this crisis.

Many years have passed since this experience. However, in a
recent retreat, I found myself once again confronted with my deep
fear of recurrence:

*I continue to bump into my inner resistance---"I'll
give you everything, Jesus but I don't want to live through
cancer again." I feel gripped by fear this morning. I know
that surrendering to the mystery of Divine Love is about
the unknown. My fear of a recurrence of cancer put me
smack in the middle of that mystery. All of this has yet
to move into my heart, into letting go, into surrender.*

*Jesus, walk with me through my fear. As I did
years ago, help me to feel deep in my soul, that no
matter what, my life is yours. Help me to trust the
movement and flow of this process as I have trusted the
flow of where you have led me this week. Ironically,
part of having trusted that flow is that all of this has
come up---again! (Journal, August 28, 2013)*

After sharing all of this with my retreat director, Fr. Norman
Comtois, I realized that my fear of a recurrence can be gift:

*My session with Norm this morning was so helpful-
--helped me put my fear in perspective --My fear keeps*

me vulnerable--more open to God and trusting God's movement within me.

--It will probably always be there because it lives so deeply within me. Talking about my cancer experience and how it has deepened my spiritual life---all the mystics had some physical issue to deal with---this is probably what led them to deeper places with God---another aspect of the body-soul connection. That touches me so powerfully!

My fear---it's more about befriending it as an invitation to surrender a bit more each time it surfaces, aware that it may never leave me completely. Also a powerful ongoing reminder of my human vulnerability---a reality I can never escape! (Journal, August 27, 2013)

My sense of God has evolved into "God as Presence" "God as Mystery" intimately involved in my life in ways I am not aware of. I often have a subtle, felt sense of God's presence in and through the events and situations of my everyday life. In quiet meditation, I often find myself drawn beneath the surface of life experience to reflect upon its meaning for my life, and to become aware of being led by the Mysterious Presence that is God. I find myself letting go bit by bit of my intellectual need to understand why things happen, surrendering a little more each time to Divine movement in my life.

This retreat also led me to look at my cancer experience differently. As I reflected on the quality of my life in the several years since my cancer diagnosis, it became clear to me that living through cancer has enriched my spiritual life:

So, so grateful for my cancer journey that has brought me where I am spiritually! I am so aware that I wouldn't be where I am without it! Cancer had to happen for me to be where I am spiritually. The gift

> *of fear coming up again, which led me to talk about*
> *my cancer experience, has made this truth very clear. I*
> *am so grateful! (Journal, August 27, 2013)*

Cancer has indeed brought me to a different place in my life. However, the fear described above is never far away. An unfamiliar ache or pain, going through a mammogram, oncology appointments, talking to someone who has had a cancer recurrence, listening to cancer patients describe what they are living---all of these experiences stir up some degree of fear and wondering. However, my fear is no longer as intense as it once was. It does not linger as long. And more importantly, I can put it in perspective.

Living the best I can, grounded in myself and in a lived awareness of the Mystery of Divine Presence has shifted my perspective and my perception of the happenings of life. Ordinary life is permeated with the sacred, with the Divine. I am invited to enter into the flow of an event or situation, being present to it as a revelation of the Divine. I have come to realize that living spiritually is a way of life that I am invited to embrace. Do I live in that place 24/7? Absolutely not. However, daily meditation and quiet reflective time incorporated into my busy days become ongoing reminders that I am immersed in Divine Mystery. It is up to me to allow that reality to permeate more and more of my life.

As we live through cancer, it is important to recognize that no one of us can change the events and situations of life. Life happens---cancer happened. The question is, how do we live what is happening? Do we force our will onto a situation? Do we become preoccupied with looking for an intellectual answer to "why" this happened? Do we put excessive energy into trying to change it? Do we hit our head against a wall to make things happen "my way?" Can we move with the flow of a life experience and allow ourselves to learn from it? Can we gradually surrender to the unfolding mystery of the events and situations of daily life? Do we live aware of being immersed in the mystery of Divine Presence?

FOR YOUR REFLECTION
AND JOURNAL WRITING

1. Spend some time reflecting on this chapter and what spoke to you. Describe what came alive in your own story as you read these pages. What touched your own experience?

2. Describe where you are currently in your recuperative process.

3. Describe how the experience of cancer has changed your life, physically, emotionally and spiritually.

4. How would you describe your sense of God as you have lived your own journey through cancer?

5. Have you blamed God for having cancer? Have you been angry with God because you have cancer? Are you afraid to admit that you might be angry at God? Honor whatever you feel, without judging or analyzing. Your feelings are part of your truth.

6. Describe your sense of being immersed in Divine Mystery. How does that truth affect your perception of your cancer experience?

CHAPTER SIX

THE GIFT OF CANCER

As I write this, we are experiencing blizzard-like conditions. Here in Massachusetts this winter, we have been measuring snowfalls in feet rather than inches, the fourth such storm in three weeks. This onslaught of winter storms is quite unusual. These past weeks have been brutal and harsh---daily routines disrupted; hours spent shoveling snow; the unpredictability of what tomorrow will bring; frigid temperatures; treacherous road conditions; the possibility of power outages; missed work days. On and on it goes. I feel snow-weary and winter-weary as February trudges on!

In the midst of this harshness, however, I can watch the snow fall and sink into its quiet stillness. The falling snow brings me very quickly into my inner core, where I appreciate its beauty. I find myself caught in the mystery of the trillions upon trillions of very small snowflakes accumulating to anywhere between one to two and a half feet with each storm. I am grateful for the warmth of our home where we can hunker down until it's safe to venture out. I enjoy wrapping myself in a comforting fleece blanket reading a book, watching a movie with my husband or sipping hot tea. I feel alive in the cold, crisp, fresh air as I shovel snow. I appreciate the quiet and leisurely pace of these days. The brutal harshness of this winter also brings the gift of unexpected time and space. There is nothing I can do about the weather except to flow with its rhythm.

As I live these days, I find myself holding both the harshness of these stormy frigid days, as well as their beauty and opportunity.

Living through cancer has been somewhat like the experience of holding both the harshness and beauty of this difficult winter. I often describe living through cancer as "going through hell and back." It was the brutally harsh winter of my life---devastating, traumatizing, shocking, terrifying, painful, difficult, confusing, challenging, anxiety-provoking, uncertain, at times debilitating. Yes, it was indeed brutal and harsh! It is not a life experience I would have chosen. But it happened. My only option was to live it the best way I could.

All these years later, I can now look back and appreciate the mysterious gift of living through this experience. Cancer has been extremely challenging, yet it has provided a new opportunity to look at my life. As a result of working through the emotional and spiritual challenges of my cancer experience, I live in greater harmony with the core of my being. I experience inner well-being and peace. I feel connected to all of creation. I have come to a new place with my sense of God and the mystery of Divine Presence that permeates our Universe as well as my life.

A WAKE-UP CALL

Life crises pull us out of our comfort zone and plunge us into the unknown. Our life, as we know it, is dramatically disrupted. We live in fear and terror. We panic. Normal coping skills tend to be ineffective. We feel lost. Nothing makes sense. We don't know where to turn. We focus on surviving, making it to the other side of the pain and turmoil and regaining some sense of normalcy in our lives.

A crisis is a wake-up call, offering us the opportunity to re-evaluate our lives, to change, adjust or tweak whatever is no longer in harmony with who we have become. A crisis is an invitation to move toward greater inner freedom and aliveness.

Living through the experience of cancer throws us back on ourselves, inviting us to look within, to re-evaluate the quality of our lives. As we move away from the shock and trauma of cancer and attempt to re-organize our life, we come face to face with what is important to us. We may need to take a look at our priorities: When all is said and done, what really matters to me? How do I want to live the rest of my life---the one precious life I have? What in my life is life-giving? What is not? What, in my general approach to life no longer works as well as it once did?

Perhaps we are workaholics who gain our sense of self and self-esteem from how much we do and how hard we work. We work long hours and take work home. We live exhausted and so wound up that we are unable to relax. Living through cancer may have helped us realize that we have neither the desire nor the energy to continue living under such pressure. Our spirit yearns for a more balanced life, but we don't know how to get there.

We may be care-takers or nurturers focused on caring for others, and unable to care sufficiently for ourselves, believing that doing so would be selfish. We may have resisted help throughout our cancer experience, believing that others have their own busy lives; we don't want to disturb them or become a burden to anyone. Yet, our heart longs for relief and for someone to be there for us.

We may find ourselves at a standstill, experiencing a need for change in our lives. Yet, we hold back, afraid of risk, of what others will say, of what our life might look like---afraid of failure. Our soul feels restless and dissatisfied. We're not sure what to do about having been pulled out of our comfort zone. We want our old life back, yet somewhere within ourselves, we sense that we cannot go back.

We may be over-responsible, taking on just about everything that comes our way, feeling we have to do it all. We often feel overwhelmed and rarely give ourselves a break. We ache for breathing space to care for ourselves, yet we feel lost with the recuperative time and space cancer provides. We don't know what to do or how to be.

Life may feel overwhelming, as we not only deal with cancer, but with financial difficulties, family struggles or tensions at work. We live stressed-out and feeling trapped. There seems to be no way out. Our entire being longs for relief.

Facing and struggling with such life issues requires the inner strength and courage to look at life-long patterns and long-held beliefs that may no longer be serving us. The wake-up call of cancer can provide such an opportunity, if we are open. We may need the help of a counselor, a therapist or a spiritual guide to accompany us through this process. Taking an honest look at our lives---where we are, what we want, what matters, is a challenge. It means that we listen and pay attention to the inner stirrings of our spirit, to our deep desires. It means having the courage to take seriously what is moving within us, honoring and respecting our inner truth, articulating it and moving toward integrating it into our everyday life.

FACING VULNERABILITY

The experience of cancer confronts us with our human vulnerability. We like to believe that we are in control of our life. We tend to think of ourselves as capable of managing every aspect of our life at all times. We pride ourselves on our independence and self-sufficiency. However, when we are hit with a diagnosis of cancer, we feel out of control. We did not choose cancer. It crashed into our lives as a most unwelcomed guest. Though we did what we could to seek the best medical care possible, we felt vulnerable, unable to control what was happening to us. Surgery and/or treatment only heightened those feelings---"What will happen next? Will I survive?"

Feeling vulnerable offers us the opportunity to move to our inner soul-place, to come to grips with our human limitations. The truth is we cannot do it all. We are not always at the top of our game. We do need help at times. We need the support of other people. For most of us, this is a difficult lesson. For many years, I have worked with and talked to many cancer survivors who felt they had to keep going. I myself experienced this same struggle. It was important to maintain a pre-cancer daily life routine. We resist listening to our energy level and honoring the reality we are living. As we explore this resistance and our drive to keep going no matter what, we may eventually realize that we are trying to prove to ourselves that, despite how we feel as a result of cancer, we can continue to do it all. We want to prove to ourselves that nothing had changed. We struggle with the unrealistic belief that we can continue our pre-cancer life-style. Eventually, debilitating fatigue and exhaustion may force us to face what we are doing to ourselves. Over time, we come to realize that cancer has changed our energy level and our life. Our human vulnerability invites us to be gentle and compassionate toward ourselves, to pay attention to the quality of our energy, to respect our limitations, to let go of unrealistic self-expectations, and to accept ourselves as we are today.

Because we live in a culture that tends to deny the reality of death, facing our mortality also makes us vulnerable. For so long, simply a diagnosis of cancer felt like a death sentence. Modern day treatments and ongoing research generally continue to prolong life after cancer. However, thoughts of not surviving or of dying from cancer are never far away. Our cancer experience invites us to face our human mortality, not in a morbid way, but as a real part of our human condition. Although our culture tends to glorify youth and good health, the truth is, someday we will die. The question becomes, "How do I want to live the rest of my life?"

The movie "The Bucket List" brings this reality to light. Aware that they have only a short time to live, the two main characters who are strangers sharing a room on the hospital oncology unit, decide that in the time they have left, and while they are still well enough to travel, they will visit parts of the world they have never seen, enjoying themselves and having fun. However, as the movie unfolds, each of the characters gradually moves within himself, recognizing those unresolved parts of their lives and eventually moving toward healing family relationships while they still have time.

What needs healing in our lives? Perhaps it is our relationship with ourselves, with others or with God. Perhaps we need to look at unresolved inner conflicts that we tend to deny or rationalize. Perhaps we carry around old wounds and hurts that we have unwittingly buried. Perhaps our experience of cancer has left us bitter, angry, depressed or resentful. The awareness of our mortality can become an opportunity to look within, to "clean house" so to speak, to move toward healing whatever needs to be healed. Undertaking this inner work leads us gradually to greater inner freedom, and the ability to flow gracefully with the rhythm of our daily life, accepting vulnerability as part of our human condition.

DEVELOPING A REFLECTIVE STYLE

Our culture lives on the fast track. We move quickly from one task or activity to another. We live "plugged in" to technology. We cannot escape our 24/7 news and information cycle that keeps us alerted to any crisis happening anywhere in the world. We are surrounded by noise and countless distractions. Our schedules are overloaded. We speed to get where we're going as quickly as possible. There is always something to do, some place to be, with little or no down time. Bedtime brings welcome relief---if we can unwind sufficiently to rest! And the next day finds us on the same treadmill. Our culture encourages us to live an outer-directed life, pulled and tugged by everything outside us, with little awareness of what is going on within.

Our outer-directed mode of living affects our approach to cancer treatment options. Because we are so stressed out, it is often easier to follow the directives of our doctors without giving them a second thought, or oftentimes, without seeking a second opinion. Paying attention to our inner reactions and giving them thoughtful consideration opens the possibility for fruitful dialogue with our medical professionals. This can result in a better understanding of, and being more comfortable with treatment choices.

Our heads are often just as busy. Our list of "shoulds" and "have tos" drives us to judge what we say and do, how we are. We are pushed by our self-expectations, which at times, can be unrealistic. We question ourselves. We wonder how we "should" be. We beat ourselves up internally if we fall short of our expectations. As cancer survivors, anxiety about whether or not treatment will work, about whether or not we've made the right decisions, about fear of recurrence, about what will happen to us---all of it swirls within us, and can become overwhelming. We may tend to play and re-play our last medical appointment. We wonder whether we understood fully what the doctor said, if we asked all the questions that needed to be asked, or if we've fully explored all our options. Our mind runs on overload, leaving us somewhat frantic and exhausted.

Becoming reflective about our life can help slow us down. It can help calm our anxieties and fears. Developing a reflective attitude means becoming more present to our everyday life experience. It means learning to pay attention to what is going on within, becoming aware of the inner stirrings of our thoughts, feelings, emotions, hunches, intuitions, desires, needs and wants. It means listening to our heart, our soul, our spirit. It invites us to respect and honor all that moves within us, without judging, analyzing or dismissing what we sense and feel. Our inner experience is part of our human reality; as such it seeks to break through our conscious thoughts. It seeks to be heard.

Living through surgery and/or treatment forces us to live differently. Slowing down holds the potential of opening us to our inner world. We have time to be present to ourselves, to listen to what is going on within. We can take the time to care for ourselves, to discover the stranger within, to connect with ourselves perhaps for the first time.

Whether or not we want to, we come face to face with what is going on within us. Our thoughts and feelings, our insecurities and anxieties, our struggle through the trauma of cancer---it's all there, at times screaming at us, wanting to be tended to. The question is, will we or won't we pay attention?

Connecting with our inner self can be frightening. We may not know the way around our inner landscape. We fear what we'll discover. "My life is fine just the way it is. I don't need to explore a world that I know nothing about. I'll get through all of this, and things will be normal again." I have often heard this and similar comments from cancer patients and survivors. When we push away inner pain and turmoil, it may be silent for a while; however, at some point, it comes back with a vengeance to haunt us, screaming at us until we have the courage to listen.

As we become more reflective about our life, we become more deliberate about our choices. We are more attentive to our energy level: "Do I or don't I have the energy to do this? Do I feel well enough? How much will this take out of me?" We tend to develop a healthy respect for our needs, wants and desires, rather than living on automatic pilot for "yes" to most requests. Perhaps for the first time in our lives, we begin taking ourselves seriously, focusing on, "Where do I want to put my energy today?"

Developing a reflective style helps us to "live today". Cancer patients and survivors too often tend to live in the future: What if this treatment doesn't work? What if I have a recurrence? What if they can't find the right treatment? Will I die of cancer? What if I can't resume my normal activity? What if I never get better? Our head can spin relentlessly with countless "what ifs"---all of which have nothing to do with today. While our concerns may be real, becoming caught up in a future we know nothing about today, keeps us agitated. We fret and worry about the unknown. Living in this future-oriented place keeps us in almost constant fear and turmoil. Although considering the future is important, we cannot live in a future that is not yet here. All we have is "today". Today we are alive.

Despite how we may feel physically or emotionally, today is a gift. How can we live "today" in a way that is meaningful and life-giving, whatever our circumstances? Our challenge is to live each today as fully as possible, without becoming excessively preoccupied with what might or could lie ahead. We can only live our life one day as a time. From a reflective perspective, each "today" is a precious gift.

Living through cancer brings us face to face with these and other life-changing realities. Our challenge is to take seriously what is stirring within us. We may be tempted to use technology as an escape. We may push ourselves, trying to get our old life back. We may run from our inner stirrings. Then we lose the opportunity to look at our life and to learn from the trauma of cancer.

As we live this process, keeping a journal can be helpful. Journal writing makes our inner experience concrete: we give written expression to what is going on inside. No longer is our inner world amorphous and vague: it is made real on the pages of our journal. Writing often brings relief from all that is swirling around inside us. It helps create a bit of distance from the immediacy of our experience, helping us to make sense of what we are living. Gradually, we become familiar with our inner world. We come to know and appreciate that part of us that may have been lost in our busy life-style or in the trauma of living through cancer diagnosis and treatment.

Over time, reflective journal writing can help us move toward a more balanced life. We begin to see our patterns. We become aware of our motivation. We gain clarity about our priorities and where we are putting our energy. We gain insight into how we react to certain situations. We learn to befriend our feelings and emotions. We become more self-aware, in a better place to make conscious and life-giving choices in our everyday life. We discover what moves and motivates us, what we are passionate about. We come to know the deep desires of our heart. Gradually, we become grounded in our inner truth, living increasingly from the core of our being, that sacred place within us where we find peace, harmony and a sense of well-being---our inner home. (For a more complete description of reflective living, see my book, <u>Reflective Living: A Spiritual Approach to Everyday Life</u>)

EMBRACING MYSTERY

The cancer experience is fraught with mystery. For the most part, we don't know why we developed cancer. Despite my own family history, I tested negative for the BRCA test, indicating that my breast cancer was not genetic. Through my reading, I discovered that only 9 to 12% of breast cancer is genetic. I had no answers. Was it environmental? Was it diet? Was it my lifestyle? Was it a combination of all of these as well as other unknown factors? I will never know. Furthermore, despite medical assurances, we often don't know whether treatment will work. We're uncertain of the side-effects. We don't know if our cancer will recur or metastasize. We don't know if we will die of cancer. We are confronted with the mysterious unknown.

While it is important that we obtain as much information as possible, and that we get the best treatment available, the truth remains that living with a diagnosis of cancer means living with the unknown, living in mystery---often for the rest of our life. Though this truth may not always be at the forefront of our awareness, it remains quite alive within our being. We need only think about our anxiety around an unfamiliar pain, or a medical test related to our diagnosis, to realize that with cancer there is no certainty. We are plunged into a mysterious unknown.

Embracing mystery is a challenge in a culture that seeks answers to everything, and prides itself in the certainty of knowing. Living in mystery demands that we shift from ego-thinking to a spiritual awareness that as human beings, our life is immersed in mystery. There is so much we don't know and will never know. As we consider our place in the vastness of the universe, we become aware that we are but limited creatures, with limited knowledge, living in a brief moment of time. This in no way diminishes our importance or the value of our life on this planet. However, our felt awareness of this larger perspective can help us embrace and live with the mystery of our particular life situation.

Embracing mystery opens the door to the Ultimate Mystery of God in our lives. As a result of our cancer experience, we may find ourselves experiencing shifts in our sense of God and in our relationship with God.

Perhaps we feel unsettled about our belief in God, questioning how God could have allowed us to be struck by cancer.

We may be disillusioned and angry that God is not answering our prayers for a cure. No matter how much we pray and others pray for us, nothing is changing.

We may find ourselves feeling lost, wondering where God is in the midst of our crisis: God *should* be there, comforting us, helping us. All we feel is absence, emptiness and darkness.

Perhaps we are confronting our childish belief in the "Magic God" who magically solves every human problem and crisis. Our lived experience may make us aware that this image of God no longer fits, but we're unsure about where to go from here. What will happen if we let go of our familiar image of God?

Perhaps God is not part of our life. We may have given up on God long ago. Or we may have never believed in God. Yet, our cancer crisis awakens and stirs God-questions within us. We are confused.

A life crisis, such as cancer often forces us to confront the God issue in our life. It can be an unsettling and confusing time. We find ourselves wanting the security of our old beliefs about God, yet feeling that these no longer make sense to us. We seek answers to our God questions. There are none.

As humans, we tend to create our own limited images of God. We want to understand this Mysterious Presence that defies our human comprehension. Our ego mind seeks to "know", "grasp", "control" a Divine Presence that is unknowable, uncontrollable and beyond our grasp.

If we are spiritually open, the experience of cancer invites us into a more personal relationship with God, as the mysterious Presence intimately involved in our everyday life---not to solve our problems or save us from crisis, but to guide us into the mystery of our own being where we find the strength, courage and resiliency to live through whatever pain and struggle we are facing.

The mystery of Jesus' passion, death and resurrection can help shed light on the God issue when we are faced with a life crisis such as cancer. In his prayer, Jesus begged God to take away his suffering. He felt terrified and discouraged. His followers were asleep and eventually abandoned him. He felt abandoned by God. He was alone and desperate, with no where to turn. God did not magically take away his pain and suffering. Rather through his prayer, Jesus found the inner courage and strength to face and live what seemed inevitable---being betrayed, mocked, humiliated and crucified. However, the story does not end there. Jesus' excruciating walk through unimaginable pain resulted in a new transformed life.

So it is with each of us as we live through cancer. We cannot be saved magically from unpredictable life events and situations. However, through our relationship with the God of Mystery we discover within the depths of our spirit what we need to walk the journey----and, over time, our life is transformed. It is important that we create time and space opportunities to nurture this mystery-dimension of life.

Soothing music, being in the outdoors soaking in the beauty of nature, walking the beach, reading, having a meaningful conversation, sipping a cup of tea, journal writing---all of these hold the potential of slowing us down and creating within us the space to BE. We may find comfort in reading Scripture, in devotional prayers, in a prayer or a Bible study group, in meditation or contemplation, in spiritual rituals. These practices nourish our spirit, moving us into the sacred inner space of our soul. There we discover that the mystery of who we are is intimately one with the Mystery of the Divine.

In the depths of our soul, we sometimes experience brief, but life-changing felt awarenesses of God's presence. We "know" in our soul that we have touched the mystery of Divine Presence. We have had an intimate experience of God. These profound experiences deepen our relationship with the God of Mystery, and give us the inner strength to continue living one step at a time, one day at a time, knowing in our heart that we are embraced by a Divine Presence that permeates us and all of creation. Grounded in our human spirit infused with Divine Spirit, we come to a soul-understanding of our cancer experience as gift.

When all is said and done, living through cancer is an invitation......

....to move toward accepting the reality of my cancer experience

....to re-evaluate my life and priorities: What really matters?

....to come home to myself

....to tap into my spiritual resources of strength, courage, and resiliency

....to listen to and honor my feelings and emotions

....to nurture my spirit

....to follow the movement of my spirit

....to develop an attitude of self-care

....to come to know and respect my inner truth

....to live differently: What is the meaning and purpose of my life at this time?

....to develop and live from a reflective spirit

....to live in harmony with who I most deeply am

....to balance caring for others with caring for myself

....to love and honor myself

....to live a spirit-inspired life

....to grow in awareness of Divine Presence in my everyday life

....to live today as fully as possible

....to rediscover my passion

....to live with a grateful heart

We cannot underestimate the power of a spiritual approach to living through cancer. In the words of Patrick Fleming,

> A deep part of us that we call soul always remains whole......Soul resilience is the consciousness that at our core there is a wellspring of energy, hope and purpose that ultimately cannot be shattered, even by the worst of traumas. (As quoted from "Ministry of the Arts Calendar," Congregation of St. Joseph, Month of February, 2015)
> **WELCOME HOME TO YOURSELF!**

FOR YOUR REFLECTION
AND JOURNAL WRITING

1. Describe what has touched you as you read this chapter. How does it affect your life?

2. Describe what your spiritual anchor(s) has/have been as you lived through cancer. How have these been helpful to you?

3. Describe how cancer has been a wake-up call for you. Describe where you find yourself in regard to shifts and changes in your life.

4. Have you allowed yourself to sink into your human vulnerability? Describe what it's like to feel vulnerable in a culture that does not value vulnerability.

5. Describe what you experience when thoughts of your mortality stir within you.

6. Where are you with God as a result of living through cancer? Describe what has happened to your sense of God through your cancer experience. Have you noticed any shifts? If so, how have you integrated these shifts into to your everyday life? If not, has your sense of God provided support through your cancer experience?

CPSIA information can be obtained at www.ICGtesting.com
Printed in the USA
BVOW08s0157140815

413254BV00001B/1/P

9 781504 336420